WORSHIP: TOGETHER WE CELEBRATE

LESLIE B. FLYNN

This book is designed for your personal reading pleasure and profit. It is also designed for group study. A leader's guide with helps and hints for teachers and visual aids (Victor Multiuse Transparency Masters) is available from your local bookstore or from the publisher.

VICTOR —————————————————————

BOOKS a division of SP Publications, Inc.
WHEATON, ILLINOIS 60187

Offices also in
Whitby, Ontario, Canada
Amersham-on-the-Hill, Bucks, England

Recommended Dewey Decimal Classification: 264
Suggested Subject Headings: WORSHIP; PUBLIC WORSHIP; RELIGION

Library of Congress Catalog Card Number: 82-62081
ISBN: 0-88207-608-6

VICTOR BOOKS
A division of SP Publications, Inc.
P.O. Box 1825 • Wheaton, Illinois 60187

Contents

To my wife, Bernice,
and to my mentor, Robert Walker,
without whose combined inspiration and instruction
I would never have authored.

Preface

Chariots of Fire, to the amazement of both secular and Christian worlds, won the Oscar for the best movie at the Annual Academy Awards in 1982. Surprisingly, the story revolved around the decision of a British runner not to compete in the 1924 Olympic 100-meter heats because they were to be run on Sunday. He then trained for the 400-meter event and came in first. How strange it is that the theme of Sunday observance was the focus in a winning film in today's Sunday-desecrating society!

A generation ago, Sunday was much more of a day of rest and worship. Perhaps the enthusiastic response to *Chariots of Fire* reflects not only the deep-down desire of a wide majority for clean movies with high ideals, but also the innate need of the human heart for a day of quiet and inner renewal through worship.

With embarrassment, I confess that only late in my Christian life have I given serious thought to the topic of worship. Vaguely I had known all during my ministry that the growing Christian and the corporate church need exercise in four directions: in worship (upward and Godward), in the study of the Word (downward and manward), in fellowship (around), and in evangelism and service (outward). As a pas-

tor, I have been involved in Bible exposition, fellowship, and outreach. But until recently I had neglected the area of worship.

Like many evangelicals raised in the free (nonliturgical) tradition, I subconsciously regarded the sermon as the chief part of the Sunday service; the rest was preliminary and peripheral. But I have come to see, much more graphically than in earlier years, that the sermon is just *part* of the worship experience. Other elements must be included if we want to worship properly. Though still a free-churcher, I deeply appreciate the variety of prescribed forms practiced by liturgical churches. We can learn much from their rituals.

My goal in this book is to lead to a better understanding and more meaningful practice of the essential elements of worship. "True worshipers shall worship the Father in spirit and in truth, for the Father seeketh such to worship Him" (John 4:23).

Do We Really Worship?

1

Dr. V. R. Edman, chancellor of Wheaton College, suffered a fatal heart attack while speaking in chapel in 1967. His topic was worship. He told how he had followed protocol in an audience with the King of Ethiopia years before. Then he likened chapel to a meeting-place between the King of kings and each student. While offering several suggestions for making chapel more worshipful, Dr. Edman's speech suddenly silenced, as he collapsed to the floor. He had entered the very presence of the King of kings.

The Almighty desires adoration for Himself and His exalted Son. But in many churches the art of worship has markedly declined. The so-called hour of worship has become a time when mind and emotions are anesthetized into neutral. Out of habit, church obligation, affection for the minister, peer pressure, family togetherness, patriotism, or community expectation, people sink into their usual pews.

Many people have never been taught how to worship. Many pastors admit receiving little or no instruction in this area in seminary. Their curriculums de-emphasized worship so that preaching and pastoral roles overshadowed priestly functions. Often pastors and people alike have no theory of worship. A great need exists today for specific education on

11

the importance, nature, and method of worship, especially in churches where worship has been displaced by "the program."

People want to worship more meaningfully. In this chapter we'll look at what's wrong with the conduct of worship, and then at what's wrong with the conduct of the worshiper.

Over-Emphasis on the Sermon

The worship hour is often called "the preaching service." The sermon is magnified at the expense of all else. The pre-eminence of the sermon stems from the Protestant Reformation in its reaction to Catholic ritualism. By emphasizing the sermon, the Reformers aimed to restore the large place early Christian worship gave to the preaching of the Bible. Even the architecture of Reformation churches, with their rectangular shapes and center-front pulpits highlighted the importance of the Word.

We should never downgrade the sermon, for by the preaching of His Word, God saves people. Sound Bible exposition nourishes the saints. But we should never focus our worship solely around the sermon. The sermon is incomplete without other worship elements, such as praise, prayer, Scripture reading, and the offering. Usually a sermon occupies less than half of the whole church service.

Lyman Beecher knew the importance of all the elements of worship. On one occasion, at the height of his popularity, he arrived late for church, ascended the pulpit with manuscript in hand, and was about to begin his sermon immediately. An elder arose, approached the pulpit stairs and whispered in the preacher's ear. Beecher climbed back into the pulpit, closed his manuscript and said, "Let us pray." After prayer, he delivered his sermon.

Sadness of the Service

Many people associate Sunday morning church with grimness and gloom, where melancholy people moan out hymns that sound like dirges. But worship is really a celebration.

Leaders should give more emphasis to joy, directing the congregation to exultation instead of dolefulness. We need more of the enthusiasm of the Salvation Army drummer boy, who was beating his drum so hard the band-leader had to tell him to lower the noise a bit. The boy replied, "Bless you, sir, since I've been converted, I'm so happy I could bust the bloomin' drum!" Of course, excitement needs to be balanced by reverence.

Sameness of the Service

For many, Sunday morning worship means not only sadness but sameness. A newcomer to town visited each church several times. He commented, "All the churches have the same order every week. At 11:10 A.M. the Baptists are always singing a hymn. The Presbyterians are always reciting the creed. And the Methodists are always chanting the 'Gloria.'"

One man whose schedule caused him to visit a liturgical church in a relative's city the same Sunday every summer, reported that he heard a sermon on the same text every year. Though the sermons varied somewhat, the Scripture was always the same—the story of the unjust steward in Luke 16.

Some churches have fostered dullness and monotony by following the same order of service, unchanged over a span of decades, meaningless to many church members. Other evangelical leaders believe it's a mistake to have a fixed order which remains unchanged from year to year. Though the general outline should be followed, the specific order of the integral parts of a service should not become inflexible. Nor should we introduce novelty simply for the sake of change. Variations should be purposeful—fitting into the unity, balance, and movement of the service.

Poorly Planned Services

Many services are thrown together with less care than a tossed salad. Hymns are introduced at certain spots just to let latecomers be seated, or the choir to march down from

the choir loft. The order wanders aimlessly with jarring transition, and with anthems and hymns unrelated to the progress of worship and the thrust of the sermon. After a sermon on temperance in which sinners were exhorted to throw their intoxicating beverages into the river, the congregation sang as the closing hymn, "Shall We Gather at the River?"

Just as a sermon requires much preparation, so does the design for a cohesive worship service. But many leaders spend only enough time on planning to pick the Scripture and hymns. The result is a haphazard mosaic. It takes forethought to weld the components of praise, prayer, Scripture, freshness, and vitality Sunday after Sunday.

Inferior Quality
The Prophet Malachi scorched the priests for sacrificing animals that were blind, lame, and sick. They offered the Lord that which they wouldn't dare offer the governor (Mal. 1:8; Deut. 15:21). Too many people bring inferior sacrifices to God's temple. They offer half-hearted singing, poorly practiced anthems, careless reading of God's Word, mindless praying, and absentminded listening to the sermon. An Australian minister, touring America, attended church in a different city every Sunday. Asked his most vivid impression of American churches, he replied, "The badness of your prayers."

Ugliness of Some Churches
Many churches are run-down buildings with dirty inside walls, messy floors, dimly lit auditoriums, dangling plaster, peeling paint, and marred furniture.

Admittedly, worship does not depend on beautiful buildings. The early church worshiped in homes, catacombs, and out-of-doors. But God, the author of beauty, puts no premium on shabbiness. Solomon's temple, blueprinted by God, was a splendid edifice, much of which was overlaid with gold, garnished with precious stones, and adorned with numerous carved figures (2 Chron. 3:6-17). Years later when

the temple had fallen into disrepair, King Joash ordered the priests to bring money for the needed repairs (2 Chron. 24:4-7). When God's house is in need of repair, He is not pleased.

When economically possible, churches should be aesthetically pleasing, not bizarre or shoddy. They should convey an aura of awe and splendor, and certainly a sense of neatness and cleanliness.

Ulterior Motives

A storekeeper who moved to a new area was advised to visit several churches over many months before choosing a home church. In this way, it was suggested, people from many churches would get to know him and possibly seek out his store.

In the Sermon on the Mount Jesus rebuked all pretense in worship. In praying we are not to stand on street corners to be heard of men. In giving we are not to blow a trumpet to attract attention. In fasting we are not to put ashes on our foreheads to advertise our spirituality. Such impure worship is not God pleasing (Matt. 6:1-4, 16-18).

The Cult of Personality and Entertainment

When Cornelius saw Peter coming to his house, he "fell down at his feet, and worshiped him." But Peter refused his worship saying, "Stand up; I myself also am a man" (Acts 10:25-26).

After the healing of the impotent man at Lystra, the people esteemed Paul and Barnabas as gods, but the apostles stopped them from offering sacrifices to them (14:11-18).

Twice the Apostle John fell at the feet of the angel who had shown him great revelations. Twice the angel forbade John, "See thou do it not; I am thy fellowservant" (Rev. 19:10; 22:8-9).

Too often people attend church to see and hear some personality. They scan the weekend newspaper for the church ads to see which church is having the best Sunday program.

Why does attendance jump when some Bible teacher, celebrity, or musical group is scheduled for a church service? The emotional and excessive adulation which some people lavish on a famous visitor sometimes equals the enthusiasm generated by an unconverted crowd for one of its idols. A few pastors, not too many, are placed on a pedestal by their parishioners. But worship is wrongly directed when the creature is honored over the Creator, who alone is worthy.

Entertainment is offered in many churches these days. Listeners could easily say to a performer, "I really enjoyed your singing," whereas they could not as honestly report, "You enabled me to worship meaningfully." We must beware lest our applause be more man-honoring than God-thanking. The spectator-entertainment syndrome must not be allowed to undercut the glory of God.

Irreverence and Inattention
In his *Journal,* John Wesley recorded how it was the custom for the gentry in many churches of his day to laugh and talk all during the service. Though most of our churches would not be characterized by noisy conversation, reverence is often missing. Loud speech, gazing all around, and visiting across the aisle are not appropriate conduct for worshipers during or before the service.

Distractions so easily destroy concentration. A mother begins to think of the dinner she has to cook. Junior wonders about that new family in the next pew. Father starts to ponder some problems at work. So he recites the Apostles' Creed with a divided mind, "I believe in God the Father Almighty" . . . *Should I turn my money-market fund into a certificate of savings?* . . . "And in His Son, Jesus Christ, who was" . . . *Maybe the money-market interest rate won't go down* . . . "suffered under Pontius Pilate" . . . *I'd kick myself if I transferred to a certificate of savings and the money-market interest rate stayed high* . . . "I believe in the life everlasting."

An epigram says, "Too many Christians worship their

work, work at their play, and play at their worship." We need to approach the Lord's presence with an overwhelming sense of awe and reverence.

Iniquity in the Life

Though worshiping the true God, the Israelites learned that at times God not only did not accept, but hated their worship. Isaiah wrote, "'To what purpose is the multitude of your sacrifices unto Me?' Saith the Lord: 'I am full of the burnt offerings of rams . . . I delight not in the blood of bullocks, or of lambs. . . . Bring no more vain oblations . . . it is iniquity, even the solemn meeting. . . . when ye make many prayers, I will not hear'" (Isa. 1:11-15).

God was displeased because the people's hands were full of blood and injustice. To make their worship acceptable they had to put away their evildoing, learn to do well, relieve the oppressed, judge the fatherless, and plead for the widows (vv. 15-17).

The evil practices of the religious leaders in Jesus' day transformed a house of prayer into a den of thieves (Mark 11:17). When James pictured a church ushering a bejewelled, well-dressed visitor to the best seat, while shunting to a lowly place a raggedly clothed man, he commented that such discrimination blasphemed God's worthy name, right in a worship service (James 2:1-7).

For six years after his conversion, John Newton commanded a slave ship. On Sundays when he would conduct worship services on board his boat, worshipers could hear the groans of slaves locked in the nearby hold. Later Newton, author of "Amazing Grace," came to realize the heinous inconsistency of such worship.

Spirit of Disunity

No offering should be made to God unless peace has been made with fellow believers. "If thou bring thy gift to the altar, and there rememberest that thy brother hath ought against thee; leave there thy gift before the altar, and go thy way;

first be reconciled to thy brother, and then come and offer thy gift" (Matt. 5:23-24).

Even partaking in the Lord's Supper can be erroneous worship, resulting in sickness and death, if taken unworthily by failing to discern the unity of Christ's body (1 Cor. 11:18, 29-30). The holy kiss, practiced in apostolic times, symbolized the peace required between believers before taking Communion. This act made it difficult for one Christian to be hostile to another. What a travesty for believers in the same service, not on speaking terms with each other, to take Communion together.

A few years ago two factions in a Connecticut church disputed over ownership of the property. When an official tried to announce the appointment of a new minister, the organist drowned him out with thunderous chords. The new minister was physically barred his first Sunday. For four years, till the court made a final settlement, both groups held services each Sunday morning, each with its own minister, one at 9:30 A.M. and the other at 11 A.M. The earlier group hurried to leave after their service, not eager to meet early arrivals for the later worship. Ironically both groups more than once repeated a prayer which included these words, "Let no pride, no self-conceit, no rivalry, no ill-will ever spring up among us."

Paul told the Roman church to glorify God with one mind and one mouth (15:6). Though members of a congregation may all recite or sing the same thing with one voice, if dissension fractures their unity then their worship will be hampered. To glorify God requires harmony among worshipers.

Vain Repetition

How easy it is for us to sing a hymn and not realize what we've been singing. Or we say, "Praise the Lord" without really praising Him. Jesus quoted Isaiah's warning against those who "draw nigh unto Me with their mouth, and honor Me with their lips; but their heart is far from Me" (Isa. 29:13; Matt. 15:8). Lip service is mockery without heart sincerity.

Jesus forbade the use of "vain repetitions" (Matt. 6:7).

Instead He gave a model prayer, the Lord's Prayer, which has been both used and abused down through the centuries. Sadly, this prayer was repeated so rapidly in medieval times that its opening word in Latin gave rise to our English word *patter. Patter* is an abbreviation of *paternoster* which means *our Father.* According to *Webster's New Collegiate Dictionary, patter* means "spiel, empty chattering talk, a quick succession of slight sounds, to say or speak in a mechanical or rapid manner, to recite prayers rapidly or mechanically."

Too often sacred phrases become Christian bywords used in mechanical fashion. The Lord's name may be taken in vain more in church than anywhere else. Some seemingly stately public worship may mean no more to God than the clack of an Oriental prayer wheel. Catch clauses, clever cliches, or ill-timed shoutings of "Hallelujah" may turn into the mindless mumblings of a Protestant rosary. The integrity of worship is diminished when we fail to pray and sing with full understanding.

Formalism—Going through the Motions

In a Protestant church in Denmark, worshipers passing down the aisle always turned and bowed toward a blank white space on the side wall. No logical reason could be given for this century-old habit. When a thorough restoration was made of the church interior, it was discovered that beneath the whitewash on the wall was a pre-Reformation mural of the Virgin Mary. The Catholic custom of obeisance to the virgin had survived 100 years of covering Protestant white wash.

Churches today face the ever-present danger that form will suffocate spirit, that ritualism will replace ritual, and that outward action will dim inward grace. Many people play at church, "having a form of godliness, but denying the power thereof" (2 Tim. 3:5). True worship must come from within, "singing and making melody" and performing all other worshipful exercises in our hearts to the Lord (Eph. 5:19).

Man-Centered Worship

Often we go to worship thinking only of ourselves and our needs. Someone said the new trinity is me, myself, and more. So many of our songs are experience-centered with words flowing manward instead of Godward. Many people go to church looking for an aesthetic experience or an emotional high. Thus they defeat the purpose by worshiping their experience instead of adoring God.

The question to ask at the end of the service is not *What did I get out of it?*, but rather *What did I offer God?* We are not in church to get, but to give. When the hymns have been sung, the creed recited, and the sermon preached, what is important is that we have uttered from the depths of our soul, "Glory be to God, and worthy is the Lamb." Of course, if the movement of the service is Godward, we can expect to receive by-products in the form of personal blessings. Objective worship brings its subjective reward in the lives of the worshipers. But worship is never realized till it loses its ego-centeredness and concentrates primarily on God.

When the body of Christ gathers for corporate worship, something significant should take place. But some of us may miss the blessing, perhaps because of one of the wrong attitudes already listed. As worshipers, we need close contact with the power of the Holy Spirit. Then, and then alone, will we worship in spirit and in truth.

What Is Worship?

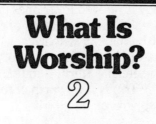

As a circus parade moved noisily through the streets of Milan, Italy an elephant suddenly swerved out of line and meandered into a church. Prancing up the center aisle and snorting every now and then, this visitor swung his trunk around, then marched back to the procession. Someone commented that many humans seem to worship like this religious pachyderm. On Sunday mornings we veer into church, make a few sounds, look around at the congregation, then move back outside to join the parade. Like elephants in church, we miss the meaning of worship.

Definition of Worship

Webster's New Collegiate Dictionary gives this definition of worship: "worthiness, repute, respect, reverence paid to a divine being." The following phrases get closer to the meaning: "man's response to the nature and action of God," "response to the glory of God," "man's response to God's revelation of Himself." "Worship is the giving to God the glory, praise, honor, and thanks due Him, both for who He is and for what He has done." Dr. R. A. Torrey said worship was "adoring contemplation of God" (*What the Bible Teaches*, Revell, p. 472).

21

Correct theology is needed for proper doxology. True worship rests on the doctrinal foundation of a holy, eternal God, transcendent yet immanent, who revealed Himself in Christ as the brightness of His glory, and who works through the power of His holy, eternal Spirit. Genuine worship relates to all members of the Trinity: the worth of the Father, the merit of the Son, and sphere of the Spirit.

The Worth of the Father

True worship is based on the inexhaustible excellencies of God. Simply, it is the acknowledgment of His insurpassable worth. The word came into our modern language from the Anglo-Saxon "weorthscipe." Shortened to "worth-ship," it was applied to a person in recognition of the good qualities or worth which he supposedly possessed. To worship God is to affirm His supreme worth, for He alone is worthy.

Two words translated "worship" are found in Jesus' rebuke when He was tempted by the devil. To the offer of all the kingdoms of the world in return for worshiping the evil one, Jesus answered, "It is written, 'Thou shalt worship the Lord thy God, and Him only shalt thou serve'" (Matt. 4:10). The first word translated "worship," *proskynein,* means literally to kiss the ground, referring to the act of physical prostration before some potentate. The second word, *latreuein,* literally "work of the people," is translated "serve." However, in other places it is translated "worship" (Acts 24:14; Phil. 3:3). When combined, these two words suggest that the true believer should first bow before the living God, then submit to God as an obedient servant.

Worship is not primarily the stirring of the emotions, or the creating of a "nice" feeling, or the liberating of the psyche. True worship is dependent on the true knowledge of God. Worship is preoccupation with God.

Dr. A. W. Tozer wrote, "The concept of the majesty of God has all but disappeared from the human race" (*The Knowledge of the Holy,* Harper, p. 123). Toward a better understanding of the glory of God he wrote *The Pursuit of God*

(Christian Publications), a study of God's attributes. Tozer advocated keeping the majesty of God in full focus in all public services.

In the Psalms, God is adulated for His person (descriptive praise), and for His work (declarative praise). Three factors that animate psalms of descriptive praise are His names, His incomparability, and His attributes.

God's power in nature should certainly elicit our worship. Two men stood on the shore watching the sun rise out of the sea, one a merchant from London, and the other the English poet, William Blake. As the bright yellow disk slowly emerged, splashing the sky with countless colors, the poet asked the merchant, "What do you see?" The merchant replied, "I see gold. The sun looks like a great gold piece. What do you see?" Blake answered, "I see the glory of God, and I hear a multitude of the heavenly host crying, 'Holy, holy, holy is the Lord God Almighty. The whole earth is full of His glory.'"

When God finished creation, He saw that it was good. Paul wrote, "The invisible things of Him from the creation of the world are clearly seen, being understood by the things that are made, even His eternal power and Godhead" (Rom. 1:20). The loveliness of nature should lead us to worship.

Some think holiness is God's preeminent attribute, while others feel that His attributes should not be ranked in importance. Stressed all through the Bible, the holiness of God has been defined as that perfection in virtue of which He eternally wills and maintains His own moral excellence, abhors sin, and demands purity in His moral creatures.

God's other attributes, all cause for worship, include His knowledge, wisdom, power, omnipresence, eternity, infinity, righteousness, faithfulness, grace, mercy, loving-kindness, love, justice, and truth. A man testified that what prepared him for public worship was the private study of the character of God. In his devotional time he would note in his Scripture reading any quality of God, then later in prayer thank God for that characteristic.

Not only do we praise God for His attributes, but for His activities as well. He answers prayer, forgives sinners, grants guidance, heals, daily loads us with benefits, protects, enlightens, and provides. We admire Him for His mighty deeds. Dr. Vernon Grounds says that worship involves awareness of God, awe in His presence, adoration of Him because of His excellencies and acts, and affirmation in praise of all He is and does.

The Merit of the Son

A little boy, turning on the kitchen radio, found a religious service. After listening a few moments, he called to his mother, "Sounds like church, but they're not saying a word about Jesus!" Any worship that leaves out Jesus Christ is not Christian worship. Our adoration must be related to the sacrificial death of Christ on the cross for our sins. Jesus Christ is the one Mediator between God and man. Through Him we have access to the Father (1 Tim. 2:5; Heb. 10:19-22; Eph. 2:18). Only those who trust in Christ's mediatorial work can worship properly.

That sinful man could approach a holy God only through a spotless substitute was repeatedly foreshadowed in the Old Testament tabernacle sacrificial ritual. The offering of the blood of an innocent goat by the high priest once a year in the holy of holies prefigured the final, once-for-all sacrifice of our great High Priest, Jesus Christ. At His death, the curtain which blocked the way into that most holy place was ripped in two to show that anyone could enter God's presence directly and boldly through Christ (Heb. 4:16; 10:19-22).

Christ is not only the basis of our worship, but the object as well. The New Testament pictures Him as possessing the qualities of deity, performing works of deity, receiving divine worship, and bearing divine names. The expression, "calling upon the name of the Lord," shows that Jesus was hailed in worship by the early church, as One worthy of adoration and surrender (Acts 2:21; 9:14; 22:16; Rom. 10:13).

Many scholars find Christ-hymns in Philippians 2:5-11,

Colossians 1:15-20, 1 Timothy 3:16, and Hebrews 1:2-4. In all of these the praise begins with His pre-existence, then moves through His humiliation and death to His resurrection and exaltation. At least three apostolic doxologies are addressed directly to Christ (2 Tim. 4:18; 2 Peter 3:18; Rev. 1:4-6). Much of our praise will be directed to Jesus Christ for His love that led Him to die on the cross, and for the joy of forgiveness, and our adoption into the Father's family.

The Sphere of the Spirit

Though a member of the Trinity, the Holy Spirit does not seem to be an object of worship in New Testament writings. Worship of, or prayer to the Spirit appears to be a post-apostolic development. It never did become very common, and occurs usually in hymns. Church father Origen taught that worship and prayer should properly be addressed to the Father, through the Son, in the Holy Spirit.

But the Holy Spirit is certainly involved in our worship. It is the Spirit by whom we worship (Phil. 3:3), who inspires prayer (Rom. 8:26-27), who opens the believer's heart and voice in praise (Eph. 5:19), who grants access to the Father through mediation of the Son (2:18), who sheds God's love abroad in our hearts and thus makes us want to praise Him (Rom. 5:5), who enlightens regarding the deep truths of God's Word (1 Cor. 2:10-16), who gives unity to a congregation (12:3-7), who gives utterance to the preacher (Acts 2:4), who teaches truth concerning Christ and thus glorifies Christ (John 16:13-14).

We must be careful not to grieve or quench the Holy Spirit lest worship be tarnished. Awareness of sin and consciousness of cleansing prepare our hearts for acceptable worship. This is why many services contain a corporate confession of sin at the beginning. "If I regard iniquity in my heart, the Lord will not hear me" (Ps. 66:18).

Not only the Holy Spirit, but our human spirits must be involved in worship. We "must worship Him in spirit and in truth" (John 4:24). True worship is a matter of the inner

spirit. Inward reality and sincerity of purpose are what count. Deep down within is where we do business with God. With our minds we understand God's character, with our wills we determine to serve Him, and with our emotions we express our love and devotion to Him.

To worship in truth is to worship consistently with the truth of Scripture, especially as it relates to Him who called Himself "the truth" (John 14:6). Interestingly, the word *orthodox* derives from two words which mean "right praise." Though the word now means "right opinion," its derivation shows that correct worship and correct doctrine go together.

To worship in truth also means to worship in a truthful way—without hypocrisy. When we play at worship—reciting a creed we don't believe, or trying to impress others—such pretense invalidates our worship and borders on blasphemy. Real worship requires truth in the inward parts.

The Need to Worship

Since we are made in God's image, the apex of His creation, we not only have the capacity for worship, but the impulse to be linked to the awesome, transcendent Power in the universe. To find fulfillment we have to worship someone or something. If we don't fill this God-shaped vacuum with Him, we will worship something else in His place—whether family, possessions, work, fame, fun, food, friends, or self. This explains the widespread idolatry at Athens (Acts 17:16), and the proliferating pluralism of religions and cults in America like ESP, the occult, astrology, transcendental meditation, and Eastern religions.

However, such strivings will never be satisfied till we are worshiping the true and living God. Augustine described man's desire for such fulfillment as the salt God puts in our mouth to make us thirst after Him. His famous dictum fits, "Thou hast made us for Thyself, and our heart is restless until it reposes in Thee." Through worship, our spiritual thirst is quenched by meeting the water of life.

When Stalin's daughter took refuge in America, she used her mother's maiden name, instead of taking the revolutionary pseudonym under which her father was known. According to the *New York Times,* her mother's name was pronounced, ah-lee-LOO-yeh-vah, a religious Russian exclamation of Hebrew origin, and pronounced in English either "Hallelujah" or "Alleluia," meaning "Praise ye the Lord," or "Praise be to God." Though Stalin professed to be an atheist, for many years he was married to "Mrs. Praise Be to God." Stalin's daughter said it was impossible to exist without God in the heart.

God wants to make worshipers out of fallen people. In His talk with the immoral Samaritan woman, Jesus said that the Father was seeking for true worshipers to worship Him "in spirit and in truth" (John 4:23). The Shorter Catechism reminds us that the true purpose of man is to "glorify God and enjoy Him forever." An early result of the Spirit's filling is worship, "speaking to yourself in psalms and hymns and spiritual songs, singing and making melody in your heart to the Lord; giving thanks always for all things unto God and the Father in the name of our Lord Jesus Christ" (Eph. 5:19-20). The people of God have been called to offer up spiritual sacrifices (1 Peter 2:5). Though we have been saved to serve, it is not so much servants God seeks, as true worshipers. God created us to bow before Him in adoration. Because the act of public worship resides at the heart of the Christian life, it has been called a matter of life and breath.

The Command to Worship
Over and over we are commanded to worship God. "Give unto the Lord the glory due unto His name; worship the Lord in the beauty of holiness" (Ps. 29:2).

"Let us come before His presence with thanksgiving, and make a joyful noise unto Him with psalms. . . . O come, let us worship and bow down; let us kneel before the Lord our Maker" (95:2, 6).

"For the Lord is great, and greatly to be praised. . . .

Honor and majesty are before Him; strength and beauty are in His sanctuary. . . . O worship the Lord in the beauty of holiness" (96:4, 6, 9).

God is to be loved by His creatures with all their heart, soul, and mind (Matt. 22:37); praised (Ps. 135:1); blessed (103:1); gloried in (105:3); exalted (99:5); feared (1 Peter 1:17); rejoiced in (Ps. 149:2); extolled (145:1); and thanked (140:13).

God's wrath is directed toward those who fail to glorify Him, but instead worship the creature more than the Creator (Rom. 1:21-25).

Not a syllable in Holy Writ suggests God's people wait until they feel inclined to worship the Most High. Rather, hundreds of times we are ordered to bring praises and thanks to God, to magnify His name, and to sing unto His name. Worship is a duty.

Only God to Be Worshiped

A wealthy man in the Orient rented his large house, but reserved one room for his gods. Placing them all in that room, he locked the door. After a long while, he came back and opened the door. He went to get his gods, but all he saw was dust. White ants had eaten them up.

Is it wrong to make images, statues, or replicas of things? No, for artistic talent comes from God. Our sin comes from worshiping the object. The second commandment could be paraphrased, "Thou shalt not make anything with the intent of worship" (see Ex. 20:4-5). Even the worship of the true God with the aid of images is taboo. Because of repeated idolatry the Israelites went into captivity, which effected a permanent cure. Apostolic preaching condemned idolatry. In Ephesus Paul's preaching destroyed the silversmith's lucrative business of making Diana-replicas (Acts 19:23-27). Early believers suffered death rather than indulge in emperor worship.

Only the one true God who said, "I am the Lord; that is My name; and My glory will I not give to another, neither My

praise to graven images" (Isa. 42:8) is to be worshiped. Since no man can serve two masters, "he that glories, let him glory in the Lord" (1 Cor. 1:31).

Response

Worship is man's movement toward God because of God's prior movement toward man. We love Him because He first loved us. God has revealed Himself extensively: in the mighty acts of history, redemption, and providence, in the loving sacrifice of His Son, in the written Word, in the giving of the Holy Spirit. God makes the first move, showing His power and love. This then invites our positive reaction of rendering exultant homage because of who He is and what He has done.

Jacob worshiped in response to the ladder vision (Gen. 28:16-22). The song of Moses flowed spontaneously after the mighty Red Sea deliverance from the Egyptians (Ex. 15). The song asks, "Who is like unto Thee, O Lord. . . . glorious in holiness, fearful in praises, doing wonders?" (v. 11) Every verse of Psalm 136 refers to a magnanimous act of God, mainly in behalf of Israel, and each verse then gives this response of praise, "for His mercy endureth forever."

Frequently Paul included praise in his letters. A sampling of these bursts of praise show they were responses to God's wisdom, power over death, deliverance from sin, to His ability to do exceedingly above all that we can ask or think, and also to His sovereignty, immortality and unapproachable majesty (Rom. 16:27; 1 Cor. 15:57; Gal. 1:4-5; Eph. 3:20-21; 1 Tim. 6:15-16).

Response after the Worship Hour

Christian worship is the *total* adoring response of the believer, not only during the worship hour, but following it as well. Worship is service. Service is worship. Thus the collection of money for the poor at Jerusalem by Paul, and the labors of Epaphroditus are both regarded as worshipful service (2 Cor. 9:12; Phil. 2:30).

In its profoundest aspect, however, worship is co-extensive with the entirety of a believer's experience. Even the beginning of the Christian life is an act of worship—for it's a response to God's love as we say, "Thank You, Lord, for sending Your Son and giving me pardon through Him." All our later acts of dedication, responding to His grace and goodness, are really worship. To proclaim God's grace is to worship. To minister to a hurting and hungry world in Christ's name is to worship. To help the poor out of gratitude to Christ is really to worship. Each deed done in response to the Father's love is an act of worship. Paul urged believers to respond to the mercies of God (outlined in earlier chapters of Romans), to present their bodies a living sacrifice, calling it reasonable service, or as in some versions, "your spiritual worship" (Rom. 12:1, NIV and RSV). True worship moves us from contemplation of God's goodness to spiritual commitment.

Together
We Celebrate
3

A pastor, calling on an absentee member, found the man sitting beside his fireplace. Asked about his absence, the parishioner replied, "I think I can worship as well alone at home." Whereupon the pastor took the fireplace tongs, lifted a live coal from the fire, and laid it down at the side of the grate. Together they watched its color and heat slowly die out. After a pause, the parishioner said, "I'll be in church Sunday."

Worship is every Christian's business. A Christian cannot fulfill his obligations in solitude. To participate with God's other children in corporate church worship is not optional, but imperative. Certainly we can worship privately in our "closets," or in our family circles, or at camps and crusades. But we must come together as a kingdom of priests to respond in praise and prayer to God.

Corporate Worship in the Bible
For Old Testament Jews, tabernacle worship was replaced by temple worship. The same sacrifices were observed in both rituals, but the splendor of temple worship far exceeded that of the tabernacle, especially after Solomon's temple was finished. One added element was the emphasis

on music. Great choirs of professional musicians provided inspiring music with magnificent instrumental accompaniment. Much of this music was introduced through the poetic-musical gifts of King David, whose inspired psalms are still an integral part of modern worship.

Jesus attended the synagogue on the Sabbath regularly, sometimes participating in the service (Luke 4:16). He used the synagogues for His teaching (Matt. 4:23; John 6:59). Likewise He was present at the three major convocations in Jerusalem (Deut. 16:16): at the Passover (Luke 2:41), at the Feast of Tabernacles (John 7:2ff), and at the Feast of Dedication (10:22).

Though the early believers had contact with the synagogue and the temple, they were ultimately expelled from both (Luke 24:53; Acts 3:1; 9:20; 13:5; 17:1-3, 10; 18:4-7; John 9:22). The early church set a pattern for corporate worship by breaking bread from house to house, sometimes in their more spacious upper rooms, praising, praying, and preaching (Acts 2:46-47; 5:42; 12:5, 12). Paul often spoke of believers coming together in the church or in one place (1 Cor. 11:17-18, 20, 33).

Most emphatically we are commanded not to neglect the regular assembling of ourselves together for public worship (Heb. 10:25).

Richness of Corporate Worship

Worshiping with others raises the voltage of spiritual faith, devotion, and commitment. In corporate worship, soul strikes soul with fire, creating a far higher spiritual temperature than possible in individual prayer. We are strengthened by the presence of others in common worship. We thrill to realize that all around the world are groups of like-minded believers, our brothers and sisters in the Lord (1 Cor. 1:2). The communion of saints turns our attention not only to contemporary fellow-believers, but to those who preceded us through the ages, helping us sense that we belong to the church triumphant as well as to the church militant.

Church attendance helps us to exhort one another (Heb. 10:25). Acts of worship stimulate courage, restore spirits, mend fragmented relationships, unify people into a congregation, and subordinate selfish gratification to the desires of the group. A major cause of the enrichment of corporate worship is the presence of Christ.

The Presence of Christ
Jesus promised, "For where two or three are gathered together in My name, there am I in the midst of them" (Matt. 18:20). This may have been a reference to a rabbinical saying, "If two sit together and the words of the Law are spoken between them, the divine Presence—the Shekinah—rests between them." But the Lord pledges that every time we assemble in His name, He is present in a way He is not present in an individual's private worship.

This added spiritual dimension makes the church service, not a take-it-or-leave-it affair, but a divinely scheduled appointment which should draw us irresistibly to corporate worship on the Lord's Day. If believers understood this, they would not decide whether or not to attend on the basis of weather, weariness, or which minister was preaching.

When we come to worship, we must believe the Lord is present. The God who inhabited the praises of Israel also joins the worship of His church (Ps. 22:3).

Do We Need a Building?
Worship demands corporate acts in a definite place. In Old Testament history God's people used buildings: the tabernacle, the temple, and the synagogues. But the New Testament says nothing about buildings for worship. Consequently many decry "budgets and buildings," claiming the church needs no structure, much less cathedrals. They say, "Surroundings do not a worship service make. If buildings are essential, the early Christians must have had poor worship. When you're really in tune with the Holy Spirit, any place will do." Others argue that with high interest rates and skyrock-

eting building costs, we should meet in school buildings or homes. They point out that the character of the people who worship in a given place determines what takes place there more than the "shape of the space." They remind us that the church may be a mud hut in Africa, a storefront in Brazil, or a cellar in China.

But after the Edict of Toleration issued by Emperor Constantine in the fourth century, a church building boom began. The new faith spread rapidly, so that bigger and bigger buildings had to be erected for growing congregations. The first Christian basilicas were rectangular with a seat at the front from which the presiding officer led the congregation in worship, preached a sermon, and presided over the Communion. Developments became more and more elaborate, finally giving us majestic medieval cathedrals. The Reformation brought a revolt against ornate ecclesiastical architecture, returning to the simple rectangular building with the pulpit at the front to stress the preaching of the Word instead of the performance of the mass.

Some today urge a return to the simple New Testament house church. They point out how the church has prospered under the Communist regime in China the last three decades by meeting in houses. But the house movement in China was a matter of survival, even as the early church's use of homes was forced upon them by persecution. It is misleading to reason that by worshiping in a house like the early church we will recapture the same spiritual power they had. Furthermore, growing congregations find it necessary to acquire some sort of permanent property and structure to carry on any worthwhile church program. However, under an oppressive government as in Communist China, the house church movement may be the only choice.

In his book, *A Place for You* (Harper & Row), Paul Tournier points out that every person needs a place—somewhere to be. Children bounced from home to home miss an essential ingredient for healthy growth. Our feelings and memories are linked to places like where we grew up, met, married,

spent vacations, buried loved ones, and became Christians. So we need a "place" for worship. Though we hear much more often about the universal church, the New Testament speaks more frequently about the local church. Of the approximate 110 times the word *church* appears in the New Testament, about 100 references are to local churches. The universal has to be localized into the church at Rome, Corinth, Ephesus. For us today the church means a place where we gather with and feel at home with fellow-believers.

Aesthetics and Symbols in Worship

Two opposite views exist on the place of art in worship: those who believe works of art have no place in church, and those who strongly hold that aesthetics and symbols have a definite contribution to make to our worship.

Those who believe the church should be void of the aesthetic point to Jesus' words about worshiping in spirit and in truth. This philosophy became prominent during the Reformation. Whereas the Lutheran stance permitted any work of art not specifically forbidden in Scripture, the Reformed churches ruled that only what the Scripture taught could be allowed in the churches. The arts in church life dropped to a low ebb as Reformers aimed at replacing beauty with drab, dreary, stark simplicity. The Reformed mentality, which called the Lutheran position "the halfway" Reformation, came to clear manifestation in the Puritans of England. In their desire to make all things biblical, the Puritans revolted not only against Catholic doctrine, but against their cathedrals and symbols. They called their plain places of worship the "meeting-houses." Some churches forbade music of any kind. Others permitted only psalms to be sung.

On the other hand, throughout the ages Christian artists of all kinds—sculptors, painters, workers in stained glass, and musicians—have used their talents to enhance worship. Magnificent cathedrals convey the majesty and transcendence of God. Steeples and soaring spires represent the idea of reaching heaven. The soft, misty light filtering through

stained-glass windows reflects the mystery and presence of God. Church bells call believers to worship. Supporters of aesthetics point to works of art in the tabernacle and the temple, such as representations of seraphim, flowers, palm trees, and pomegranates. Garments made for Aaron's sons were "for glory and for beauty" (Ex. 28:40). All of these required men endowed with a Spirit-given art ability (31:1-11).

Which view is right: artist or iconoclast? Perhaps each has value. For those who advocate art, two dangers exist. First, we may mistake an aesthetic response for a spiritual experience. Second, the artistic may woo us from the real to the transient, the sensate thus seducing the soul.

On the other hand, any work of art that would help us worship spiritually without becoming a crutch would be appropriate. When the Reformers, though with much provocation, stripped their churches bare of anything that might appeal to the imagination and the aesthetic sense, they went too far.

They forgot that a symbol is a visible sign which helps us understand spiritual reality. They also seemed to forget the rich heritage of symbolism from Christian history. Many early Christians could not read, so learned through symbols, which also provided a rallying point for loyalty to Christian truth. Evangelicals today could profit from a survey of symbols used by Christians through the centuries. For example, the Father is represented by a hand reaching out of a cloud, or by an all-seeing eye. The best known symbol of the Son is the fish, whose five Greek letters stand for Jesus, Christ, God, Son, and Saviour. One symbol of the Spirit is the flame, another the descending dove. The Trinity is represented by an equilateral triangle, or three interwoven circles. The Bible is portrayed by two tablets, an open book, or a lamp.

Whether we worship in a simple building or some lovely sanctuary, it's the heart attitude that invests the place with true exaltation, and makes it the haven for the presence of Christ.

Celebration

Joy, an essential ingredient of worship, does not receive as much emphasis in some services as it should. People would more likely connect "loud cymbals" (Ps. 150:5) with a youth concert rather than with a dignified Sunday morning service. Too often worship hours degenerate into a dullness that makes people think of God as a grouch. The way a congregation sings may be the barometer of its spiritual health.

Old Testament worship was full of exhilaration. We read, "Make a joyful noise unto the Lord. . . . Come before His presence with singing" (Ps. 100:1-2). The Israelites considered the worship of God a cheerful privilege. Why should we shout ourselves hoarse at a football game on Saturday, and turn cold and lifeless on Sunday morning when we consider the impact of the Gospel? We should find some excitement as we rejoice over God's love and pardon.

When Mel White became the new minister of a small Covenant church in Pasadena, California he wanted a sense of exultation the first Sunday to match his theme, "Celebrate, You've Been Pardoned." Two large banners were created to hang on either side of the wooden cross over the pulpit. They depicted Miriam and two women picking up their timbrels and dancing to celebrate the crossing of the Red Sea. Outside ushers wore large buttons with "Celebrate" on them, instead of the usual white plastic carnation. The bulletin cover was bright yellow. A large paper banner with "Let's Celebrate" hung from the bell tower. A brass ensemble played hymns on the front steps. Though the service contained the usual elements, no one was bored. Week after week people came with the feeling, "I was glad when they said unto me, 'Let us go into the house of the Lord'" (Ps. 122:1).

Praise

The dictionary defines praise as commendation, or expression of approval. Basically it means to show admiration, extol, laud, be boastful or excited in joy. Secularly, it would

be the shout of triumph when your favorite baseball team has just won, or you have just received a coveted award. Spiritually it means loud, eager acclamation of God's amazing goodness and grace.

All Hebrew terms for praise suggest a public and vocal expression of delight in God. Whereas thanksgiving may take the form of silent and private recognition, praise openly tells what God has done for you. The forceful word *hallelujah* simply means "praise the Lord."

Some other Old Testament verbs in the vocabulary of praise include "bless" (Ps. 103:1-2), "sing" (92:1), "make a joyful noise" (95:1), "extol" (145:1). The Hebrew title of the Book of Psalms is *Praises*. Psalms serves as the textbook on praise which is to be offered in the assembly of the righteous (149:1).

J. B. Phillips, who gave us a New Testament translation by his name, spent an evening with soldiers in a service center in London. After a few hours of fun and fellowship, he suggested they close with worship. One soldier piped out, "We haven't any idea what 'worship' means." Phillips replied, "It's three cheers for God." Much of the celebration in worship takes the form of praise, sometimes even raucous praise.

Not Spectatorism

Worship is not a spectator sport. Everyone celebrates. All too often the pulpit monopolizes the service, diminishing interest on the part of worshipers. The philosopher Kierkegaard likened worship to a play in which the congregation has not gathered to watch a performance, but to become active participants in the drama. The people are the actors, while God is the audience. He said ministers and choir leaders are prompters who cue worshipers in to their lines as needed, giving words of response to God, and clothing them with the emotional accompaniment of music. Too often in our services the actors sit apathetically, while the prompters do all the lines to try to keep the play more lively. But who likes drama in which the prompters do all the work? The

up-front folks are not to entertain us, but to lead.

Paul's description of a Corinthian church service indicates that almost everyone contributed something to it (1 Cor. 14:26). For several centuries worship was mainly clergy-directed. The Reformation tried to restore the congregation's voice in the service. The publication of the Church of England's *Book of Common Prayer* aimed at greater laity participation. It's title shows worship was to be for everyone commonly, or for the community.

Even when a section of the service is led by a person up front or by a choir, we need not sit back as spectators, certainly not as critics. Rather, we should look beyond any deficiency of content and style, identify with as many of the prayers and hymns as possible, and creatively make them our own adoration and petition. Even when an anthem is poorly sung, we should do our best to hear its message. Instead of evaluating the merit of the sermon and the creativity of the preacher, we should listen expectantly. Teddy Roosevelt used to say, "Even though the preacher can't preach for sour apples, and the choir is more than a half note off-key, you can always get something out of worship if you will put yourself into it."

Dialogue—The Rhythm of Worship

Many church services are virtual monologues by the up-fronter. But worship is meant to be two-sided. In the rhythm of worship, God takes the initiative by revealing something of His attributes and actions. Then the believer responds. Essentially, worship is dialogue. God speaks; we answer Him. God speaks again; again we reply.

Examples of this pattern are found in Scripture. Jacob's ladder was a two-way escalator, with angels descending and ascending. God spoke to Jacob, giving a promise. Jacob responded with a vow (Gen. 28:12-22). Here is the flow of revelation and reply, proclamation and prayer, heavenly promise and earthly vow.

In Isaiah's vision, first comes a revelation of God's majesty

and holiness, followed by the prophet's response of confession of sin. Then ensues God's cleansing and call to service, to which Isaiah obediently surrenders (Isa. 6:1-8).

It has been said that God speaks to us through the reading of Scripture and the sermon; then we respond through hymns, confession, dedication, and prayer. But often revelation and response interfuse in the same worship element. Many psalms are both God's word to man, and man's prayer to God. Hymns, likewise, can be a form of revelatory truth, as well as responsive praise. Even though perceiving these phases of simultaneity in certain categories of the worship service, we best celebrate corporately by maintaining the dialogue between God and man. Thus our orders of service should reflect rhythm of divine awesomeness and human acknowledgment.

Congregational Participation

Since the total church should share in the worship celebration, as many people as possible should be involved in the service. Congregational activity can be encouraged through responsive calls to worship, corporate confession of sin, responses to prayers, and responsive, antiphonal or unison Scripture readings. Some churches use a litany, which is a series of invocations or supplications, each one followed by a short prayer, like "Have mercy upon us," or "Good Lord, deliver us." Sometimes people hand in prayer requests, written on slips of paper which are read from the pulpit, one at a time, each followed by silent prayer. Liturgical churches call these "Bidding Prayers."

The saying of Amen after hymns, prayers, creeds, and at other appropriate times, has both Old and New Testament precedence (1 Chron. 16:36; 1 Cor. 14:16). Fourth-century Latin church father Jerome said that at times the noise of the Amen sounded like the crack of thunder.

I'll never forget the Congress on Evangelism in Minneapolis in 1969 when Dr. Harold Lindsell asked the thousands present to stand and pray out loud whatever was on their

heart. Though conscious of a babble of voices, I found the experience moving. Later I learned that this way of praying is practiced by many church groups around the world. Still other churches appoint three or four laymen in advance to pray, or if the acoustics are good, open the service for volunteer prayers from the congregation.

The Physical Side of Worship

A man said, "The prayingest prayer I ever prayed was while I was standing on my head." He had fallen down a narrow well, head-first, and was tightly wedged in. Though the Bible does not require specific actions for the various parts of worship, certain postures have developed through church history, often with scriptural suggestion.

Kneeling has been the accepted position in petitioning prayer, with heads bowed and eyes closed. The psalmist appealed to us to "kneel before the Lord, our Maker" (Ps. 95:6). Our Lord knelt in Gethsemane, even falling on His face (Matt. 26:39). Till the last half of the 17th century, the Reformed churches of England and Scotland knelt for prayer. During the 18th century, the independent churches made sitting for prayer a much more common practice. The large First Baptist Church of Dallas, Texas has kneeling units for all its pews.

When Dr. J. Oliver Buswell was president of Wheaton College, he often led in prayer in the chapel service with his eyes open toward heaven. Historians tell us that standing with eyes open was often a Jewish posture for prayer.

The standing posture shows respect in offering praise to God. Many have held that though we sit for the sermon, we should stand for the reading of the Bible as did God's people in Nehemiah's day (9:4-5). Standing at the benediction may signify the believer's intent to live out the Gospel in obedience. In fact, the Council of Nicea forbade any believer to kneel on Sunday, because only by standing could believers declare the victory of the Resurrection. In the same vein, the processional march, suggestive of Palm Sunday and Good

Friday, is a formal movement leading to the public worship of God, whereas the recessional march symbolizes believers going back out into the world.

References to religious dancing are scanty in the Old Testament (Pss. 149:3; 150:4). Miriam led the women with timbrels, song, and dance in thanksgiving for the marvelous deliverance from the Egyptians (Ex. 15:20). David danced before the Lord with all his might when the ark of the covenant was brought to Jerusalem (2 Sam. 6:12-15). Since no record exists of any dance in connection with apostolic church worship, evangelicals are not likely to include this exercise in their Sunday morning services. However, many congregations, taking their cue from David's choir (Ps. 47:1) clap their hands during spirited singing.

Praying with hands outstretched was an Old Testament custom (Pss. 134:2-3; 141:2). John Calvin stated in his *Commentary on the Book of Psalms* that it has been a common practice in all ages for men to lift their hands in prayer. This habit has been revived by Christians in recent years. The upraising of hands may express either the receiving of blessings or the presenting of petitions in faith.

Bodily movements are not necessarily acts of worship, nor do they guarantee that their significance will automatically occur. Unless the spirit is lifted to the Lord, actions will be mere conformity to custom. Yet we must not overlook the potential reciprocal relation between bodily action and soul faith. Through physical movement, commitments can be made, vows declared, and the challenge of faith accepted.

As we go to worship, our hearts should be filled with sincerity, intensity, and fervency. When we can join the psalmist in saying, "I will praise Thee with my whole heart" (Ps. 138:1), then together we'll celebrate.

Why Sunday?

A book, *The Weekenders,* points out that the weekend in America is the nation's moment of hope. Every Friday evening a national transformation takes place as people head home for two days of respite from their jobs. Affluent Americans make an exodus to lake cottages, ski resorts, or recreational parks.

The book also reports some stimulating ways people spend their weekends. For example, a pretty secretary performs stunts on the wings of a speeding biplane before an admiring crowd. A life insurance salesman wades for hours with his two boys in icy streams, panning for gold. Another family uses weekends to trace its family tree, visiting scenes that played a part in their ancestral history.

Though much initiative goes into weekend planning, one major omission sticks out like a sore thumb. Never is any suggestion made that people ought to attend worship services. Sunday has become a national holiday instead of a holy day. It has been said that our great-grandfathers called it the Holy Sabbath; our grandfathers, the Sabbath; our fathers, Sunday; but today we call it the weekend. And many think it is getting weaker all the time.

Weekend vacations have markedly decreased Sunday wor-

ship attendance. One church in Minnesota, wishing to switch rather than fight this weekend lifestyle, changed its Sunday worship to Thursday evening. This permitted people to have an uninterrupted long weekend.

Is it necessary to worship on Sunday? Why Sunday?

Sunday Is a Special Day

Sunday is the only day singled out in the New Testament for unusual emphasis. All four Gospels record the Resurrection on the first day of the week (Matt. 28:1; Mark 16:2; Luke 24:1; John 20:1, 19). The following Sunday, Jesus appeared to Thomas. No other event in the Gospels is so connected with a particular day as is the Resurrection of Christ. So it's not surprising that on the first day of the week the disciples met in honor of His victory over death.

Paul instructed the Corinthians to bring their offering for the poor in Jerusalem "upon the first day of the week" (1 Cor. 16:2). Probably they had already been holding meetings on the first day of each week. Since similar advice was given other churches (v. 1), we deduce that Sunday worship was a widespread practice.

Enroute to Jerusalem ending his third missionary journey, Paul met with the believers at Troas for worship, instruction, and the Lord's Supper on "the first day of the week" (Acts 20:7). Though Paul was there for seven days, no mention is made of any service on any other day, not even on the Saturday-Sabbath. The verb "came together" in verse 7 is the common word for assembling in church meetings, and gives us our English word *synagogue*. Among those assembled were converted Jews, who formerly "synagogued" on Saturday, but who now "synagogued" on Sunday.

The first day of the week is called "the Lord's Day" by the Apostle John. The beloved disciple, banished to the desolate Isle of Patmos, and meditating on spiritual matters on the first day of the week, was given a vision of his glorified Master. He wrote, "I was in the Spirit on the Lord's Day" (Rev. 1:10).

Missionaries tell us that Moslems faithfully observe their stated days and times of prayer, even when quite ill. Though their prayer exercises require much physical movement, they perform the prescribed motions at all five periods of daily prayer, always facing Mecca. Should not those who profess to know God through Jesus Christ honor Him with their physical presence on the day repeatedly and distinctively underscored as "the first day of the week"?

Sunday Replaced the Sabbath
The institution of the Sabbath can be traced back to creation (Gen. 2:1-3). Because no other mention is made till the giving of the Law at Sinai, many conclude the Sabbath was not observed till then. But others claim that the Sabbath was more or less observed for over 500 years from Sinai to Elisha without mention (Deut. 5:15—2 Kings 4:23). The command, "*Remember* the Sabbath day" (Ex. 20:8), seems to point back in time, giving support to the view that Sabbath observance was part of creation ethics, binding on mankind from the beginning.

The question comes, "Is the Sabbath commandment binding on believers today?" The Synod of Dort in 1619 said, "In the fourth commandment of the Law of God there is something ceremonial, and something moral. The resting upon the seventh day after creation and the strict observance of it, which was particularly imposed upon Jewish people, was a ceremonial part of that Law. But the moral part is, that a certain day be fixed and appropriated to the service and the holy meditation upon Him." A similar concept was stated in the Westminster Confession of 1647.

These statements acknowledge a continuing moral principle in the fourth commandment that can still be applied to today's believers. Dr. Nelson Bell wrote, "The Ten Commandments have never been abrogated. It is still wrong to kill, to steal, to commit adultery. . . . To deny the validity of one day in seven as a day of rest and spiritual refreshment is to miss one of God's greatest gifts to mankind" (Leslie B.

Flynn, *Now a Word from Our Creator,* Victor, p. 64). To rule out completely one of the Ten Commandments from the practice of the New Testament, while the other nine are repeated in it, seems to fragment the Decalogue.

But the ceremonial aspect of this commandment is annulled. The Sabbath was a special sign between God and Israel (Ex. 31:16-17). The New Testament, after Pentecost, never enjoins the observing of the Sabbath. No verse in any New Testament epistle commands Sabbath-keeping, nor is Sabbath-breaking ever included in any list of sins. Violations of all other nine commandments, such as idolatry, disobedience to parents, murder, adultery, stealing, false witness and covetousness, are spelled out as sins, but never Sabbath-breaking.

Of the nine post-Pentecost references to the seventh-day Sabbath, eight speak not of a Christian gathering, but of a strictly Jewish service, which Paul attended for the purpose of evangelizing (Acts 13:14, 27, 42, 44; 15:21; 16:13; 17:2; 18:4). The ninth reference declares the Christian's liberty from Sabbath and observance of feast days. To those in the Colossian church who contended for a Christian keeping of the Sabbath, Paul advised in plain language, "Let no man therefore judge you in meat, or in drink, or in respect of an holy day, or of the new moon, or of the Sabbath Days" (Col. 2:16). Paul also rebuked the observance of "days, and months, and times, and years" in the Galatian epistle as the error of returning to weak and enslaving elements (4:9-10).

Some people say it doesn't matter which day of the week we worship on. They quote Romans 14:5 for their support: "One man esteemeth one day above another; another esteemeth every day alike. Let every man be fully persuaded in his own mind."

However, Charles Hodge suggested that the phrase, "one day above another" refers to special festival days, not days of the week (*Commentary on the Epistle to the Romans,* William S. Martien, p. 318). In the church at Rome one group of believers still celebrated Jewish feasts, including the Sab-

bath, but a second group held only to Sunday worship. Hodge inferred that both groups worshiped on the first day of the week, but differed as to whether Jewish holy days should be kept.

Paul taught that both groups, equally desirous of serving the Lord, should be tolerated, since the veneration of days was a secondary issue. In the interest of harmony, each group was allowed to follow conscience, some keeping just Sunday, others both Sunday and Jewish feasts, including the Sabbath.

Christians today are no longer required to observe the Sabbath. But if we're convinced of the permanence of God's moral law, then the principle of setting aside one day in seven still applies. Certainly an important part of its observance would require the assembling of believers for worship, preferably on the first day of the week.

Celebration of the Resurrection
Everybody loves a holiday. Some holidays are tied to a season like Thanksgiving, others to historical events. But Sunday is a holiday that is observed in many nations. For 2,000 years believers have commemorated the first day of the week. Why?

The early church met on the first day to celebrate the glorious resurrection of Jesus Christ from the dead. At first terrified and unbelieving, they slowly realized that their Master had triumphed over the grave. That happened when He met with them that first Sunday evening behind closed doors. Again, the next Sunday Jesus met with them. They were so convinced of His power over death that they soon filled all Jerusalem with teaching about the Resurrection. And they continued meeting on the first day of the week, unable to forget the thrill of that first Sunday.

At first many continued synagogue worship on Saturday, and temple prayers as well, along with the first-day assembly. Soon persecution and conscience discouraged Saturday synagogue and temple observance. Then Sunday evening

became the focal point of worship, involving both agapé (love-feast) and the Lord's Supper. Sunday morning service was also begun, permitting slaves to worship before going to work.

Ample documentary evidence indicates that the early church observed the first day of the week. Ignatius, writing around A.D. 107 to the Magnesians, said, "They who walked in ancient customs came to a new hope, no longer living for the Sabbath, but for the Lord's Day, on which also our Light arose" (Chap. 9). Pagan historian Pliny, governor of Bithynia A.D. 111-113, in a letter to the Roman emperor Trajan, referred to Christians as meeting on a fixed day before daylight and reciting responsively among themselves a hymn to Christ as a god.

The most complete description of a church service from the middle of the second century comes from Justin Martyr's *The Apology*. Writing to explain the "strange beliefs and practices of the Christians," he described a Sunday worship service. "On the day called the Feast of the Sun, all who live in towns or in the country assemble in one place, and the memoirs of the apostles or the writing of the prophets are read as time permits. Then, when the reader has ended, the President instructs and encourages the people to practice the truths contained in the Scripture lections. Thereafter, we all stand up and offer prayers together; and as I mentioned before, when we have concluded this prayer, bread and wine and water are brought. Then the president likewise offers up prayers and thanksgivings according to his ability, and the people cry aloud saying Amen. Each one then receives a portion and share of the elements over which thanks have been given; and which is also carried and ministered by the deacons to those absent" (*The First Apology of Justin Martyr*, LXXVII).

Not till the time of Constantine in the fourth century did Sunday become the official day of rest from work. Sometimes the accusation is made that Constantine changed the day of worship from Saturday to Sunday. But the day had

already been changed. He only put official approval on a day which had been observed as the day of worship for some 300 years. Saints in all centuries have celebrated the Resurrection on the first day of the week. Pondering that great victory, we look back to God's finished redemption which has brought spiritual rest. We also look forward to the day when a fallen creation, now groaning, will receive its redemptive rest through the saving work of Christ (Heb. 4:1-11; Rom. 8:19-23). On Sundays believers witness to their contemporaries both what Christ has done and yet will do.

Sadly, many celebrate the Resurrection only once a year. On Easter they dress up and go to a sunrise service or a morning worship hour to join the crowds honoring the victorious Christ. Yet the Resurrection is not to be commemorated just once a year, but every week. Churches should be jammed every Sunday for a weekly jubilation.

The pastor of a Nebraska church advertised in the local newspaper in the lost-and-found column after a slump in church attendance the Sunday after Easter. The ad read:

LOST OR STRAYED—About 250 church attendants who were last seen on Easter Sunday, but were not to be found the Sunday following. No questions will be asked if those returning are willing to have their Easter zeal every Sunday.

Our lives need an every-Sunday meeting with God. A mother who took care of her children only every other week would not qualify as a good mother. A man who was faithful to his wife on alternate weeks would be guilty of infidelity. So those who attend church spasmodically, even two Sundays a month, are not faithful to their obligation of weekly worship.

On the contrary, many believers are consistent in their Sunday attendance. A news item from Oklahoma was headlined, "What's the Matter with Mrs. Esperito?" It told how this 61-year-old lady had not missed church in over 1,000 Sundays, a perfect record for nearly 20 years. Then it asked these questions:

Doesn't she ever have company to keep her from church? Doesn't she ever have headaches, colds, nervous spells, tired feelings, sudden calls out of town, business trips, Sunday picnics? Doesn't she ever sleep late on Sunday mornings? Doesn't it ever rain or snow, or get hot or cold? Doesn't she ever get her feelings hurt by the preacher or by some member? Doesn't she have a job to keep her away? Doesn't she have places to visit over the weekend (the only time she has)? What's the matter with Mrs. Esperito anyway?

Reasons for Sunday Worship

The Lord is not pleased when His professed followers don't attend church (Heb. 10:25). If believers are to obey this command to worship corporately, they have to know where and when to meet. Thus, through the centuries, believers have designated special places for services like chapels, churches, and sanctuaries, and specific times like Sunday morning and evening.

Some have held that we are free to select any day of the week instead of Sunday. But also realizing that total freedom to observe any day could lead to keeping no day, they saw the need for appointing a particular day, thereby preserving order, reverence, decency, and peace in the church.

But what day would they select? From apostolic times the church almost universally has adopted the first day of the week for Christian worship in honor of Christ's resurrection, so Sunday was the logical choice. To have a specific day when God's saints assemble as a congregation to praise, pray, and hear God's Word gives a rhythm to worship which fits the ancient pattern of six days to work and the seventh to rest.

If a church did decide to have its main worship service on Thursday evenings, this would not invalidate its worship. But perhaps the church could also maintain a Sunday service in order to help preserve a day whose sanctity and influ-

ences are fast fading. Perhaps Christian people could encourage the scheduling of social and recreational events so as not to conflict with church worship.

Blessings of Sunday Worship

We should come to church to bless God, not primarily to get a blessing. But in blessing God, we get blessed so that we leave the service with a deep sense of personal uplift. Though worship has the objective purpose of glorifying God, it produces a subjective benefit in the worshiper.

The apostolic church owed much of its power for godly living and heroic dying to the truth and inspiration derived from public worship (e.g., Acts 4:31). Also the public service was the springboard for much evangelism and missionary enterprise, such as the commissioning of Barnabas and Paul (Acts 13:1-3).

Worship strengthens. It is impossible to have contact with the living God without an increase of soul vigor. Empty spirits are filled. Eyes are fixed on Christ. Attitudes are improved. Material interests are subordinated to spiritual values. Joy is expanded.

According to a study of 189 middle-aged men who had died of heart trouble in a three-year period in a Western Maryland community, a John Hopkins University medical research doctor discovered that the risk of fatal heart disease was almost twice as high for men who attended church infrequently than for those who attended once a week or more. The doctor also observed that the "clean life" associated with regular church-going also appeared to be statistically related to a less likelihood of becoming ill with a dozen other major illnesses.

Church attendance contributes to a higher degree of mental health. People today are in trouble, mixed up, and in need of direction, so they turn to tranquilizers, drugs, alcohol, radical lifestyle, the occult, perhaps suicide. Though a weekend at the ocean or historical site may be somewhat therapeutic, a real source of help can be found in the inspiration

and instruction of a genuine worship service. Dr. Hudson Armerding, Wheaton College president, commented, "Perhaps the mental and emotional illness that plagues even the Christian community might be lessened if men deliberately set aside the pressures and tensions of demanding schedules and devoted one day in seven to meditation, worship, and fellowship. Like the other nine commandments, the fourth is designed to enable man to serve his Creator better" (Leslie B. Flynn, *Now a Word from Our Creator,* Victor, p. 71). Sunday is the day that sees us "safely through another week."

Church attendance joins us with others who hold the same beliefs and ideals. Church attendance also provides spiritual instruction. After a poor sermon one church member said to another, "Almost a waste of time." To which the reply came, "If the preacher doesn't know his duty, I thank God at least I know mine."

An elderly lady who worked hard washing floors six mornings a week was on her way to Sunday morning worship. A friend who knew how hard she worked asked, "Wouldn't it be better for you to sleep late on Sunday mornings? Wouldn't that help you keep going?" The old lady exclaimed, "It's going to church on Sunday that keeps me going the other six days of the week!"

Church attendance has a cleansing effect. A vital connection exists between what happens on Sunday and what occurs the rest of the week. The result of a vertical relationship with God in corporate worship should spill over in our other relationships through Spirit-empowered ministry to others. In its broad aspect, worship includes not only divine service on Sunday, but during all of life as well.

Liturgy or Liberty?

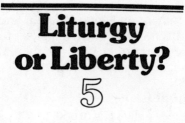

In a little town the Presbyterian and Methodist churches wanted to unite into one church. But they couldn't agree on how to say the Lord's Prayer, whether "Forgive us our trespasses," or "Forgive us our debts." So the newspaper reported that the Presbyterians went back to their trespasses, and the Methodists to their debts.

Churches have varying orders of service, involving a structure of hymns, prayers, responsive readings, and other verbal formulas which they follow regularly. This formalized succession is called liturgy.

The word *liturgy* comes from two Greek words meaning "people" and "work." Its roots go back to Greek city-states where people would devote time to jobs like building bridges, or repairing roads as a service to the community. Its meaning progressed to the more sacred obligation of service to God and His people. Ecclesiastically, it now has the idea of "the way people customarily do things," or "worship style," or "order of service," or "structuralized ritual," or simply the form of spoken words and symbolic movements by which we channel our public devotion to God.

Churches exhibit wide variations in worship style, some simple, others sophisticated. On the one hand we have the

liturgical denominations which follow a fixed, rigid pattern. On the other extreme, reacting against set forms like written prayers and recitation of creeds, are the free churches who eliminate all but the basics of worship.

History of Liturgy

No order of service is prescribed in the New Testament. However, Paul's description of a service at Corinth indicated a high degree of spontaneity as various people contributed a psalm, a teaching, a message in tongues, a revelation. On this informality Paul imposed certain restrictions, affirming that God is not the author of confusion but of peace, and commanding, "Let all things be done decently and in order" (1 Cor. 14:40).

The first documentary evidence of any pattern of worship comes from a letter written by Justin Martyr around A.D. 150 in which he described a service as having singing, praying, Scripture reading, sermon, offering, and the Lord's Supper. At this time worship seems to have been free and informal, though prepared prayers were occasionally used.

As time went on, a preference for formality became evident. Prayers became fixed forms to be recited or read. Less stress was placed on the reading and preaching of the Word, and more on the Lord's Supper which developed into the Mass. The Mass became something done by the priesthood which the congregation merely watched. The almost exclusive use of Latin, not generally understood by the people, made worship less meaningful to the common man. This drift continued for over 1,000 years. Many other practices were also introduced, such as regard for relics, veneration of martyrs, wearing of vestments, rosaries, and stations of the cross. The 12th century saw the start of the withholding of the cup from the laity in the Mass. Monasteries developed a daily regime, called offices, to be observed corporately throughout the day and night. Some monastery prayers found their way into public services.

Another factor contributing to the formalization of wor-

ship was the need for uniformity and regularity in large assemblies, especially after Christianity became the official empire religion. Later, the invention of printing technically made possible the imposition of uniform worship by ecclesiastical authorities who controlled their area.

During the Reformation, Protestant leaders worked to reinstate preaching to a place of importance, restore the Lord's Supper to its original simplicity, and to return the service back to the people in their own language. Church leaders introduced the phenomenon of congregational singing. Luther and Calvin became the founders of a high literary style in their respective countries of Germany and France through their compositions, prose and poetry, to aid the public worship of the commoner.

Though the Reformers agreed in principle that the focus of Sunday worship should be the preaching of the Word rather than the Lord's Supper, still the Communion service retained a very important place in worship. Luther and Calvin urged the Supper be observed every week, but Zwingli's view that a complete worship experience was possible without Communion finally held sway within Protestantism. So the Protestant worship hour tended to become a preaching service.

The Lutheran and Reformed traditions tended to adhere to formalized structures and model prayers. In England the more radical believers broke away from the established Church of England, emphasizing informal worship. Known as Separatists (or the Free Church) they rejected all established liturgical forms. Their services included only prayer and the exposition of Scripture. Prayer was always spontaneous. Not even the Lord's Prayer was used.

At the time of the Reformation the people of England longed to worship in their own tongue. To help them, *The Book of Common Prayer,* a comprehensive worship book written in English, was printed. Though most Christians are fairly familiar with the *King James Authorized Version* of the Bible, not many evangelicals have read through *The Book of Common Prayer.* Making its official appearance in January

1549, *The Book of Common Prayer,* with minor revisions, is used by the Anglican (Episcopal) church today. Interestingly, almost every man who helped arrange the book died a martyr. Also, the first Christian service held on the North American continent was read from this book.

The Book of Common Prayer has its roots in antiquity. It represents the accumulation of the best devotional exercises of previous centuries. It contains all 150 Psalms and the Apostles' Creed, which dates back to the fourth century. Because the first prayer book was essentially a Catholic book, revised editions toned it down to a more Protestant position. When he broke with the Anglican tradition, John Wesley edited for the use of his followers an abridgment of *The Book of Common Prayer.* Many other denominations use service books for worship.

Written Prayers

Many evangelical Christians have strong feelings against the practice of reading or writing prayers. These advocates of spontaneous prayer might be surprised to learn that Jesus undoubtedly used the Jewish prayer book when He attended the weekly synagogue service. The day He participated in His hometown synagogue worship by reading from Isaiah 61, He most likely conducted the opening devotions which included the reading of a couple of prayers (Luke 4:16-20).

Some object to written prayers because people repeat the same prayers over and over. But the proponents of spontaneous prayer fall into the same practice, for most people who lead in prayer usually lapse into usage of habitual word patterns.

Not only do spontaneous prayers become as stereotyped and formal as written prayers in words, but also in content. The average worshiper in a free church can almost anticipate what his minister is going to say in his prayer, as he moves from the sick and sorrowing to the shut-in and burdened, then on to those in authority, then to the missionaries of the cross, and so on. People who use some book of

written prayers are forced to break out of their limited circle of interests to a much wider range of needs.

Liturgists are quick to point out that free churches use written prayers every Sunday. Many hymns are really prayers put to music, like "More Love to Thee" and "Take My Life and Let It Be." If it's possible to sing a prayer-hymn composed by another and mean it, why can't we read a written prayer and mean it? Furthermore, if we use the old favorite hymns over and over, why should we criticize those who use the same prayers repeatedly?

If people who are called on to pray publicly could listen to themselves, they would probably be shocked at their disconnected phrases, bad grammar, poor word choice, redundancy, meandering, and even mild blasphemy by overusing God's names. How rude and rambling they would sound in comparison with the eloquently expressed pleas found in *The Book of Common Prayer.* Of course, beauty of language doesn't impress the Lord, but neither does verbosity and incoherence.

Most Churches Have Liturgies

Once a congregation comes together for worship, the people must follow some sort of sequence. Otherwise, every person doing his own thing creates bedlam. Because some general agreement must exist as to what to do and when to do it, a ritual develops.

Someone protests, "But in our Gospel-preaching church we worship as the Spirit leads us." But repeated visits to that church will reveal an order of service as fixed as in any liturgical church. First, it's the "Doxology," then an invocation, then a hymn, followed by a prayer, an anthem, announcements, offering, another hymn so the choir can march down from the choir loft, the sermon, the closing hymn, and the benediction. The sequence does not change from week to week, nor from year to year. Any deviation would discomfort the congregation and suggest borderline heresy.

When a Baptist preacher started the service one Sunday

morning with the pastoral prayer instead of a hymn, his deacons later informed him they would have no innovations. Ironically, these deacons who protested liturgy were binding their pastor with their own form of liturgy.

The New Testament Order of Service

Is there a correct order for a worship service which should always be followed? The New Testament contains no specific "church order," however some hints are given. The New Testament teaches that disordered worship is offensive to God. When Corinthian church worship became chaotic, Paul instructed, "Let all things be done unto edifying" (1 Cor. 14:26). Then he proceeded to lay down regulations to correct the situation, in the midst of which he said, "God is not the author of confusion, but of peace, as in all churches of the saints" (v. 33). Then he summed up, "Let all things be done decently and in order" (v. 40).

God is a God of order—in the universe, in the setting up and transporting of the Old Testament tabernacle, in the human body. We should not be surprised that through the centuries conscientious Christians have aimed to express their gratitude through ordered worship. Though no one particular arrangement can be affirmed as the true and only way, some ordering is both proper and essential. Otherwise, haphazard worship may fail to edify the saints.

New Testament Worship Based on Synagogue Worship

However minimal the elements of New Testament worship, they grew out of synagogue worship. The synagogue sprang up during the Exile to help God's people maintain their identity through the reading and expounding of the Law.

By the time of Christ, synagogues were everywhere in the Mediterranean world. They were the place of public worship. Christ attended the synagogue. Paul's missionary work began regularly in the synagogues of the Dispersion. New believers, both Jews and proselytes, came from synagogues. Thus it's not surprising to find features of synagogue wor-

ship in the early Christian church. New believers likely formed synagogues of their own, only with a Christian emphasis, at first meeting in homes with large upper rooms. When James spoke of "your assembly," the word was literally *synagogue* (2:2).

The four major elements of synagogue worship carried over into New Testament worship are: praise, prayer, Scripture-reading, and preaching.

Praise. Praise opened the synagogue service. The Talmud laid down the principle, "Man should always first utter praises, and then pray." Perhaps this is why "a psalm" heads the list in the description of Corinthian worship (1 Cor. 14:26). The early church sang (Eph. 5:19; Col. 3:16).

Prayer. Synagogue prayers included the Shema, "Hear, O Israel, the Lord our God is one Lord" (Deut. 6:4). Then followed 18 petitions covering a wide range of themes, both spiritual and material. The early church was known for its praying in public (Acts 2:42; 1 Tim. 2:1-2). Like the Hebrews in the synagogue, the early Christians uttered a genuine Amen at the end of the praying (1 Cor. 14:16).

Reading of Scripture. The synagogue service followed a fixed order of Old Testament reading. The Pentateuch was read through in three years. Lessons from the Prophets were also read, all translated into the vernacular of that area. Visitors were invited to do the reading. The day that Jesus read the Scripture in His hometown synagogue, He was handed the scroll of Isaiah. Likely when He opened it, "He found the place" which had been assigned for that day (Luke 4:17).

The public reading of the Word became a standard part of early church worship (Col. 4:16; 1 Thes. 5:27; 1 Tim. 4:13). In fact, most New Testament epistles were written for reading in a particular church or group of churches. As they were circulated, they were given great emphasis, taking their place alongside the Old Testament.

Preaching. The homilies in the synagogue service were more didactic than exhortatory, often taking the form of Targums (condensed explanations of the Scripture read).

Any person in the assembly, judged fitting, was invited to deliver the sermon. This was why Paul preached in so many different synagogues (Acts 17:1-3). Of course, his instruction was eagerly anticipated in Christian assemblies (20:7).

New Testament church services also included the *offering* (Rom. 15:26; 1 Cor. 16:1-2; 2 Cor. 9:10-13) and the *Lord's Supper,* which were not derived from the synagogue, but directly from the Upper Room. The two major parts of the weekly service could be characterized as the sermon (stemming from the synagogue), and the Supper (stemming from the Upper Room).

The Order of Service

John Skoglund in *Worship in the Free Churches* points out that the parts of the service described by Justin Martyr and discussed in the preceding section of this chapter are "maintained in all the great liturgies of the church. . . . The same essential elements are found in the rites of Chrysostom and Basil in the East, the Gaelic and Roman masses of the West, the orders of worship developed in the Reformation by Luther and Calvin on the continent, and the English *Book of Common Prayer*" (Judson Press, Valley Forge, p. 38). In other words, these are the basic elements of worship everywhere in Christendom.

A typical, moderately liturgical Sunday morning order of service might look something like this:

Prelude
Call to Worship
Hymn (or "Doxology")
Confession
Hymn of Thanksgiving
Old Testament Lesson (or Responsive Reading)
Apostles' Creed and Gloria
New Testament Lesson
Pastoral Prayer and Lord's Prayer
Anthem
Hymn

Sermon (preceded by Prayer for Illumination)
Collects (Short Prayer)
Offering
Hymn
Communion (if to be observed)
Benediction

The Church Year

The church year is the history of redemption in vertebrate form. As followed by liturgical churches, the first half of the church year goes from Advent (Sunday nearest November 30th) till Pentecost (seventh Sunday after Easter). The second half begins at this juncture with Trinity Sunday and takes up the rest of the calendar till the Sunday before Advent.

The Advent season, which proceeds from Advent Sunday through Christmas Eve, focuses on the coming of Christ. Christmastide commences Christmas Day and ends Epiphany Eve, January 5th. These days depict the Incarnation and hope of salvation in Jesus Christ. Epiphany season starts January 6th and continues through the eve of the third Sunday before Lent. The main theme of Epiphany is the manifestation of Christ to the Gentiles as they were symbolized by the Magi's visit. More recently, stress has been placed on missions.

After a three-week preparatory period, Lent (which begins on Ash Wednesday) provides a time of self-examination, penitence, and rededication. Passiontide, the two weeks of Lent ending with Palm Sunday, is followed by Holy Week.

Eastertide, beginning with Easter Sunday, and extending through Ascension Day and Pentecost, emphasizes the exaltation of Christ, which culminates in the birth of the church at the descent of the Holy Spirit.

Then comes the second half of the church year, from 23-27 Sundays, depending on the date of Easter. This long section is termed Trinity or Kingdomtide, stressing the believer's response to God in discipleship and service.

No one knows how the church year came into existence. The Reformers took opposite attitudes toward it. Though Lutheranism retained the general outline by celebrating its more important festivals, Calvinism observed only the Lord's Day, discarding all others because of lack of scriptural justification and danger of superstitious implication. But as late as a century ago, Easter and Christmas were not observed by many churches. The American Sunday School Union carefully avoided any reference to Christmas in its lesson materials till 1859, so controversial was the issue.

Today most evangelicals in free churches follow the major aspects of Christ's life—Christmas, the Passion, and Easter—planning messages around the Incarnation, sufferings, and Resurrection.

Liturgy or Liberty?

Baptist preacher Charles Haddon Spurgeon once said that he would sooner risk the danger of a tornado of religious excitement than see the air become stagnant with a deadly formality. But practitioners of free forms of worship may easily slip into an informal liturgy just as deadly. Does true worship have to be either passionless ritualism or unstudied informality?

Liturgies have their place. Like the Sabbath, liturgy is for the people, not people for the liturgy. Many traditional forms possess timeless vigor and a natural eloquence, which can hardly be improved upon. These were not first framed for people to follow; rather they grew in the matrix of church worship, and later generations followed. Liturgy is what the church says, not what the church is told to recite.

Regrettable loss is suffered by abandoning the church's devotional heritage. Liturgical forms may have a stabilizing effect by deepening faith, articulating adoration, strengthening the will, and reinforcing doctrine. The liturgists also say the prescribed lectionary readings will cover far more of the Bible in public services than is covered in the average free church.

Spontaneity is needed. Standardized liturgy runs the risk of losing its vigor and becoming mechanical. Some people crave the freedom of informal worship services.

Reserving the right to occasionally depart from a printed order of service, when the Spirit leads, gives a satisfying sense of flexibility. Interestingly, the opening paragraph of the preface to *The Book of Common Prayer* states that in the worship of Christ, different forms and usages may be allowed without offense, provided the substance of the faith be kept. Its standard, general prayers may be altered to meet common needs.

Balance Between Liturgy and Liberty

We need both order and spontaneity. Today many liturgical groups are infusing life and warmth into their traditional forms of worship, transforming them into living liturgy. On the other hand, many free churches are beginning to appreciate the dignity and value of prescribed structures, incorporating pertinent elements into their own services.

The Scriptures neither require the use of prescribed forms of worship, nor do they forbid liturgy. Perhaps in the early church, worship was mostly spontaneous. Later forms developed so that free or fixed expressions were suitable. We do know that the medieval church suffered so deeply from standardized modes of worship that the Reformation dealt not only with doctrine, but with worship as well.

Perhaps we could call the combination of liturgical and nonliturgical services "optional liturgy." This combination has several advantages. It coincides with the ideals of the New Testament, culls out the best traditions of the centuries, and conserves all the benefits of free worship by permitting God's people to express their devotion extemporaneously.

In a sense liturgical worship looks back to the old ways of worship. But "optional liturgy" opens the door to spiritual adventure, as worshipers look forward to new ways of expressing adoration of the Triune God.

Combining Liturgy and Liberty

Many churches are trying to put new life in their services. A chief preoccupation seems to be how to make worship "creative." However, we must not innovate just for the sake of doing something different. New approaches should be made with sensitivity.

The Worship Committee

Many pastors, instead of taking sole responsibility for the order of worship, have enlisted the expertise of their ministers of music. More and more today, pastors are also inviting the laity to participate in the ministry of worship within the bounds of authority.

For example, services at College Hill Presbyterian Church in Cincinnati, Ohio are planned by the worship team of laypersons who have studied worship and feel a call to this area of church life. Meeting twice monthly, the group first of all worships, then individual team members meet with the pastor to discuss a particular service assigned them, and to hear the thrust of his sermon for that day. Then fitting musical numbers are selected in consultation with the minister of music. Attempts are made to maintain balance between structure and spontaneity.

Visit Other Churches

A Christian college student related how after years of free, evangelical-type worship, something was missing in her life. Her interest in church dwindled. In this state of mind, she walked into Westminster Abbey on a trip to England. There in a service in that majestic cathedral, her attention was directed to the holiness of God.

She said, "I began to taste what worshiping can mean. . . . I do not believe the Church of England or any denomination has the last word on worship. I am not calling Baptists to become Episcopalians or the evangelical church to canonize its leaders and learn Latin. . . . But perhaps we have rejected liturgical worship so categorically that we are afraid to

kneel. As a result, we have forgotten who God is, and we think we can pat Him on the back. I worshiped God in many different ways before I went to England. But I had reached a point where my mind was cluttered with Sunday School bulletins and youth group activities, and I had lost sight of God's greatness. My experience with formal, structured worship helped me refocus on the One I was worshiping" (*Moody Monthly,* Oct. 1978, pp. 63-64).

On the other hand, an Episcopalian rector met regularly with a small group of interdenominational believers for Bible study, sharing, and singing. Leaving one of their meetings, he headed for an Episcopalian ministers' meeting. Arriving excitedly, he exclaimed, "I've found a great hymnbook!" It was a Gospel songbook, *Tabernacle Hymns Number Three.*

Explain Changes
People are willing to accept changes if they understand what's happening. This keeps surprises from becoming shocks. Leaders should always explain in advance when they plan to do something differently.

One Sunday a preacher decided to include the kiss of peace, an ancient part of Christian history with New Testament authority. But the practice was new to the congregation. The innovation offended two families so much that they left the church because of "such indecencies." Had the pastor explained the significance of the custom in advance, this unpleasant result probably could have been avoided.

Dr. Abe Van Der Puy, of radio station HCJB, sums it up well, "We should keep away from the inflexible, purely routine, coldly formal type of service, as well as from the other extreme which becomes irreverent. Rather we should be open to the Spirit's guidance with an emphasis upon *freedom* as well as on *order.*"

A Good Start

At one time when tyrants ruled over China, a summons to appear in the emperor's court in Peking's Forbidden City made strong men tremble. Any visitor was expected to perform the required complicated kneelings and prostrations faultlessly. The slightest violation could bring a sentence of instant death. To gaze at the emperor was forbidden. To speak out hastily was fatal. On receiving a call from the emperor, Chinese officials frequently said their last farewells to their families, so slim were their chances of surviving a royal audience.

How different for the child of God who is invited to come boldly to the throne of his King, to "obtain mercy, and find grace to help in time of need" (Heb. 4:16). However, it is possible for us to abuse our entrance rights. The reminder to "serve God acceptably with reverence and godly fear, for our God is a consuming fire" (Heb. 12:28-29) helps us seek a balance between familiarity and reserve.

Worship Requires Preparation
Because believers are participants in worship, we should come prepared. Wouldn't people attending a play be irked if the actors arrived late for the performance? And wouldn't

they be more irritated if the cast had not practiced their lines? The audience would be angry because they paid the regular price to get in. Since God paid the supreme price of His Son's blood, should not worshipers arrive on time Sunday mornings?

Saturday Night

One man recalls his Saturday night ritual as a boy. He polished his shoes, set out his Sunday clothes, took a bath, and studied his Sunday School lesson. His practice has biblical roots. The *Preparation* was a technical term in the Gospel narratives indicating, first, the evening of Friday, then later the entire Friday (Matt. 27:62; Mark 15:42; Luke 23:54; John 19:14, 31, 42). Ostensibly, the devout would use the period immediately prior to the Sabbath to prepare their hearts for the day of rest and worship.

The Scottish poet, Robert Burns, in his *The Cotter's Saturday Night,* describes the peasant family's preparation for the coming Lord's Day. Convinced of the importance of preparing one's heart before entering the Lord's house, the Puritans made much of Saturday night. Calling it the "Vigil," they used the imagery of warming the oven of one's heart on Saturday night by reflecting on the majesty of God, so that upon arising Sunday the oven could be easily kindled in devotion.

Perhaps the answer to reanimated worship is not some catchy innovation, or drastic change of order, but in hearts renewed through preparatory heart work.

Before the Service

Just as Old Testament priests washed their hands before entering the tabernacle, so believers today need to examine their lives for any need of cleansing (Matt. 5:23-24).

The psalmist wrote, "Who shall ascend into the hill of the Lord? Or who shall stand in His holy place? He that hath clean hands, and a pure heart; who hath not lifted up his soul unto vanity, nor sworn deceitfully" (Ps. 24:3-4). Other moral

prerequisites are added in Psalm 15, such as speaking truth, not backbiting, not harming one's neighbor, and keeping one's vows.

We should go to worship with as few distractions as possible. Whatever dominates our thinking—whether sports, money, business, friends or worries—should be surrendered to God. We may even have to offer the honest plea, "Lord, You know I don't feel like worshiping today. But You want me to, and I must. Warm my heart to sing Your praises."

To go with the right attitude may mean a reasonable bedtime Saturday night, and rising early Sunday morning. Rushing around the house at the last minute creates family friction and destroys worship anticipation.

Entering the Service

Perhaps exchange of greetings could be reserved for the hallways or lobby. Once inside the sanctuary, we should cease chatting. It's a good idea to arrive a little early. Landing in the pew just as the minister starts the service will distract others.

Once in our seats, we should pray silently. As the organ plays, we can concentrate our thoughts on God. We should ask the Lord to tune us in to His interests in the worship service.

Leadership Has Responsibility

The pastoral staff certainly bears some responsibility for the preparation of worship. To properly lead the congregation in praise of the Triune God requires advance thought.

The minister or staff should instruct the congregation in the meaning, importance, purpose, and means of worship. Some people have gone to church for years without really developing their worship muscles. The leader should provide the spoken directions (rubrics) so the congregation can understand the significance of what they are about to do, as well as its relationship to what has preceded and to what will follow.

Call to Worship

Prepared hearts will welcome the call to worship. But for those coming from the informality of a Sunday School class, or from a family feud which erupted before church, the call to worship will be a needed reminder of the vertical dimension of life.

The Bible furnishes many ready-made calls to worship. For example, Psalm 95:1-3 could be used:

O come, let us sing unto the Lord: let us make a joyful noise to the rock of our salvation. Let us come before His presence with thanksgiving, and make a joyful noise unto Him with psalms. For the Lord is a great God, and a great King above all gods.

Other possibilities include Psalms 34:1-3; 100; 103:1-5; Isaiah 40:28-31; and Jeremiah 33:2-3.

One church's secretary often types out several call-to-worship sentences and places them in the bulletins. The special bulletins are handed to early arrivals who are alerted to the numbered enclosures. At a prearranged signal, the person with number one rises and reads his call to worship. Then spontaneously the others rise in succession, sharing their verses with the listening congregation.

We are the ones who need to be called from our inattention and diversions. God is already waiting for our worship.

A Sense of Awe

Awe is an essential element in true worship. Transcendent wonder at God's majesty gives a sense of inadequacy on the part of the worshiper, whose weakness stands in vivid contrast to the infinite might of God.

Translators around A.D. 1000 spoke of God as "awefull." Through common usage the graphic term gradually degenerated till it applied to any situation causing awe. By 1800, with spelling modified, it came to mean "exceedingly great." The once-potent word for holy reverence is now debased to such phrases as "awful weather" or "awful pain." The Septuagint (Greek version of the Old Testament) translated

awful as "fearful, terrible, dreadful." In its verb form, to awe means to fear reverently.

Awe characterized Bible characters' worship of God. Abraham fell on his face in holy wonderment when God spoke to him (Gen. 17:3). The morning after Jacob's ladder vision, he exclaimed, "Surely the Lord is in this place. . . . And he was afraid, and said, 'How dreadful is this place! This is none other but the house of God'" (28:16-17).

At the burning bush the Lord told Moses, "Draw not nigh hither; put off thy shoes from off thy feet, for the place whereon thou standest is holy ground. . . . And Moses hid his face; for he was afraid to look upon God" (Ex. 3:5-6).

The Israelites trembled at Mount Sinai, learning that God should not be approached casually or carelessly (19:16). When Ezekiel saw "the likeness of the glory of the Lord," he fell on his face (1:28).

Isaiah wrote:

> In the year that King Uzziah died I saw also the Lord sitting upon a throne, high and lifted up, and His train filled the temple. Above it stood the seraphims: each one had six wings; with twain he covered his face, and with twain he covered his feet, and with twain he did fly. And one cried unto another, and said, "Holy, holy, holy, is the Lord of hosts: the whole earth is full of His glory." And the posts of the door moved at the voice of Him that cried, and the house was filled with smoke (6:1-4).

The fear of the Lord is not only the beginning of wisdom, but of worship too. But reverence is lacking in many church services today. The late Dr. A. W. Tozer felt that far too many believers hold a superficial view of God, resulting in emasculated worship through failure to ascribe to Him His proper magnificence.

When Alfred Smith was governor of New York, he agreed to attend a convention banquet. On arrival he discovered that the mostly non-New York audience had a disdainful attitude toward him, regarding him as some sort of joke. The

toastmaster introduced him somewhat disrespectfully, "And now I give you that great guy, Al Smith." Sensing a slight to his position, the governor made his point quickly. He told how as a little boy he had been taken to see a great civic parade. Holding his father's hand tightly, he watched as battalion after battalion of soldiers marched by. Suddenly his father straightened up. Young Al felt tingling pride. Immediately his father ordered, "Son, take off your hat. The Governor of New York is passing by." He told how he took off his hat. Then Smith gave his punch line, "Gentlemen, the Governor of New York bids you good night." And he walked out the door.

Could there be occasions when God Almighty walks out of our congregations because we have approached Him with the casualness of a pal, instead of with the fearsomeness that befits Him? A renewed sense of His overwhelming splendor will help us to be "lost in wonder, love, and praise."

Silence

A period of silence can help remind us that "the Lord is in His holy temple" (Hab. 2:20). One Sunday a church in California arranged to have the congregation enter the morning service in complete quiet. Though announcement had been made the previous week, ushers whispered a word of reminder. No prelude broke the silence. (Some thought the organist was ill, or the organ needed repair.) Most people prayed or read their Bibles.

Many liturgies have a place for corporate silence. But silence is a dimension of worship which must be carefully planned, for people often feel uncomfortable, even embarrassed, by silence. How does silent prayer fit in with the total direction of the service? How long will it last? Without suitable instruction the silence can be deafening. Some appropriate times are prior to the worship hour, before or after the pastoral prayer, following the benediction—the latter ideal for solidifying the thrust of the sermon. Such slices of quiet can enrich worship.

Confession of Sin

Though many believers have been brought up in churches which never incorporated a confession of sin in their services, the practice has historic precedent.

In *Whatever Became of Sin?*, Karl Menninger says that the early Christian church cells were composed of small groups who met regularly, sometimes secretly, with an order of service which included self-disclosure and confession of sin. Confession was followed by an announcement of repentance and plans for restitution. This ritual continued till Emperor Constantine made Christianity the official state religion and instituted private confession to a priest, which was later depersonalized by the use of a confessional box. Though the Reformers eliminated the confessional, they did emphasize direct confession to God, and included a corporate confession of sin in their public worship.

The prayer of confession in the *Book of Common Prayer* is a classic:

> Almighty and most merciful Father: We have erred, and strayed from Thy ways like lost sheep. We have followed too much the devices and desires of our own hearts. We have offended against Thy holy laws. We have left undone those things which we ought to have done; and we have done those things which we ought not to have done; and there is no health in us. But Thou, O Lord, have mercy upon us, miserable offenders. Spare Thou those, O God, who confess their faults. Restore Thou those who are penitent; according to Thy promises declared unto mankind in Christ Jesus our Lord. And grant, O most merciful Father, for His sake, that we may hereafter live a godly, righteous, and sober life, to the glory of Thy holy name. Amen.

Corporate confession has its dangers. We need to be brought face to face with our sins as individuals, not as a crowd. Also, we must be careful not to let the routine repetition of words become meaningless. To combat this, some

churches observe a period of silence after the general prayer to permit private, specific searching and repentance. At other churches people are asked to take a piece of paper inserted in the bulletin and write down some fault they wish eliminated from their lives. Then they place their unsigned papers in a container passed through the pews. The leader announces that the papers will be burned, then offers a prayer seeking divine help for these resolves.

After the prayer of confession the leader voices the assurance of God's forgiveness. Many in the congregation, burdened with guilt, need to be reminded of God's matchless grace which fully and freely covers our sins. Perhaps a hymn of pardon could be sung, or a penitential psalm could be read. Psalm 51, David's great prayer of confession and pardon, is particularly fitting. The announcement of pardon could include verses of forgiveness like 1 John 1:7, 9; Romans 5:20; or Ephesians 1:7.

Announcements

Ideally, announcements should be printed in the bulletin so members of the congregation can read them at their convenience. It seems time-wasting for the minister to read what people already have before them. But some meetings will require special emphasis.

Making announcements and greeting visitors before the call to worship clears the way for uncluttered worship. Some pastors who feel that announcements disrupt the flow of worship, make all announcements near the start of the service—perhaps after the prelude, but before the formal worship begins. Saving the announcements till the end tends to dissipate the sermon's effect.

Announcements should be read carefully before being read out loud. When read to the church they should be stated briefly, clearly, and only once. Notices that do not apply to the whole congregation should not be made in the corporate service. Announcements should be judiciously worded.

Warm Spirit

To offset cold architecture, echoing ceilings, and circulating drafts, a church needs bright lights and cheerful people. Not only should the doors of the church be open, but the doors of the members' hearts as well.

Friendliness is everyone's job, not just the ushers'. One man, asked why he joined a certain fellowship, explained, "I had no sooner got comfortably seated than a child in the next pew handed me a hymnbook, then a man beside me put a Bible in my hand, and the minister looked at me as though he had seen me before, and was glad to see me again." Some churches reinforce their friendly welcome with a coffee hour in the church parlor for all visitors after the service. A prepared heart, a friendly spirit, a suitable treatment of the announcements, a call to worship that brings a sense of awe at God's majesty, and a confession of shortcomings in the light of our holy God: all these elements will help get a worship service off on a right start.

Psalms, Hymns, and Spiritual Songs

7

A prominent American clergyman gave several reasons for opposing newer trends in church music. For example, it's too new. It's often worldly, even blasphemous. The new Christian music is not as pleasant as the more established style. Because there are so many new songs, you can't learn them all. It puts too much emphasis on instrumental music rather than on godly lyrics. This new music creates disturbances, making people act indecently and disorderly. The preceding generation got along without it. It's a money-making scheme. Some of these new music upstarts are lewd and loose.

These observations sound like modern criticism of present-day Christian rock and folk music. But the comments were written in 1723 by a minister who opposed the introduction of a new, threatening menace known as hymn-singing. (From article, "What's Wrong with the Beat" in *Christian Life,* by Michael Wilshire, Feb. 1981, p. 28. Footnote says, Thomas Symmes, "A Joco-Serious Dialogue Concerning Regular Singing, 1723, in History of Church Music")

Several years earlier a 20-year-old youth had attended a chapel in Southampton, England where the singing was deplorable. A clerk read out a crudely rhymed psalm line by

line. After the reading of a line, the congregation sang it, then waited for the next line. Scarcity of tunes made for monotonous droning. Since hymns of human origin were ruled out because allegedly God's Word could not be improved upon, only psalms were allowed.

After church the youth complained to his father about this "doggerel double distilled." His father retorted, "Give us something better, young man!" Accepting the challenge, he came to the non-conformist chapel the next Sunday with his first effort, a hymn which has maintained its loveliness to this day,

> Behold the glories of the Lamb
> Amidst His Father's throne;
> Prepare new honors for His name,
> And songs before unknown.

His composition met with such approval that many Sundays he brought new hymns to chapel. In 1707 he published the first real hymnbook in the English language, *Hymns and Spiritual Songs*. Termed the "father of English hymnody," Isaac Watts introduced the style of hymn singing now prevalent in today's churches.

Music—The Language of the Soul
Though described as "a people of the Book," evangelicals are really a people of two books—the Bible and the hymnal. Since music is the language of the soul, it is natural for worship to employ hymns accompanied by instruments.

Poetry, by itself, informs and enchants. It can reach areas of the mind seemingly inaccessible to logic, and arouse responses of reverence and devotion which few sermons could evoke. When music is added to poetry, the combination may enhance, inspire, dramatize, teach, and emphasize.

Music is not only an act of worship, but an aid to worship as well. The singing of Isaiah 9:6 in Handel's *Messiah* ("His Name shall be called Wonderful, Counselor, the Mighty God, the Everlasting Father, the Prince of Peace") makes a great

emotional impact. Since a hymn or choir number may cause truth to live, or move us more deeply than the sermon, church music has been called "the younger brother" of the preacher.

Music in the Old Testament

Early Scripture describes Jubal as "the father of all such as handle the harp and organ" (Gen. 4:21). After rescue from the Egyptian army, the Israelites, safely across the Red Sea, burst forth in a song of deliverance (Ex. 15:1). Just before his death, Moses was ordered by the Lord to write a song for his nation, rehearsing God's goodness plus warning against backsliding after entering the Promised Land (Deut. 31:19—32:44). Deborah and Barak sang praise to the Lord for His rescue of Israel from the Canaanites (Judges 5).

By the time of David, professional guilds had been established "to be the singers with instruments of music, psalteries and harps and cymbals, sounding, by lifting up the voice with joy" (1 Chron. 15:16). Skillful leaders were appointed. David's interest in Israel's music program is frequently mentioned (6:31-32; 9:33; 13:8; 16:4-43).

Imagine the sound of music when the ark was brought into Solomon's finished temple, for the celebration involved 288 singers, furnished with cymbals, psalteries and harps, and 120 priests sounding with trumpets, all united "to make one sound to be heard in praising and thanking the Lord . . . saying, 'For He is good; for His mercy endureth for ever' that then the house was filled with a cloud, even the house of the Lord" (2 Chron. 5:13). Music was involved in all of Israel's major revivals. Ezra (3:11) and Nehemiah (12:24, 31) indicate a well-ordered arrangement for responsive singing between two choirs at the restoration of the temple after the return from Exile.

Interestingly, the longest book in the Bible is a book of music, the psalter, the inspired prayer and praise book of Israel. The English word *psalms* is a transliteration of the Greek title of the book, *Psalmoi.* The Greek word originally

meant a striking or twitching of the finger on a string, and grew into the idea of "pulling or playing a stringed musical instrument." The expanded meaning is "sacred songs sung to musical accompaniment."

Dealing more with experience than with theology, the psalms run the gamut of every mood from deepest despair to adoring delight. Though a believer can learn to pray in the psalter, praise is its real theme. No matter how bad the hurt at the start of a psalm, the latter half always leads to praise. The entire book is a goldmine for hesitant lips and stammering tongues to use in prayer and praise.

Music in the New Testament

Four canticles are found in the nativity and infancy preface to Luke's Gospel: Mary's *Magnificat,* Zachariah's *Song,* the angels' *Gloria in Excelsis,* and Simeon's *Nunc Dimittis.* Anna's adoration likely took the form of a song though its contents are not given (Luke 1—2).

The church was born in song. Unable to remain silent in the newfound joy of the Good News, believers praised God daily (Acts 2:46-47). But what did they sing? The psalms. Not only did the psalms contain devotional language, but they foreshadowed Christ in ways He explained to the apostles in the Upper Room (Luke 24:44). But because the psalms left out much distinctive Christian belief, hymns and spiritual songs were added to early church worship. Paul commanded both the Ephesians and Colossians to use psalms, hymns, and spiritual songs in their singing (Eph. 5:19; Col. 3:16).

Scholars believe that some portions of the New Testament possess hymn potential because they are written in a poetic pattern. For example, 1 Timothy 3:16 falls into six lines of rich truth concerning the person and work of Christ. A series of couplets, in which the second line complements the thought of the first line, present the Gospel message through Christ's ministry. Many think these verses were an early church hymn. Other passages lending themselves to the

same pattern include John's prologue (John 1:1-14), called the "Logos Hymn," also Philippians 2:6-11 and Hebrews 1:3.

Purpose of Christian Music

Church music has been called a functional art, existing not so much for its artistic value, but for its usefulness in the service. Four major purposes of music are: to worship, teach, encourage, and evangelize. Church music should also reinforce the doctrines of the church. Ambrose, a fourth-century bishop in Milan, wrote hymns with the deliberate intent of spreading orthodox teaching in the face of Arian heresy. Many Reformation hymns helped impress on the Protestant consciousness that salvation was by faith alone.

Another goal of church music is to encourage one another. As a priesthood of believers we are all to exhort, build up, express care, and strengthen one another through hymn-singing. Though music is not listed as a spiritual gift, it is a glorious vehicle for the exercise of gifts like evangelism, teaching, and encouraging.

Survey of Church Music

Music in the apostolic church seems to have been totally congregational. As the church grew, congregational singing fell into disrepute, and was outlawed by the Council of Laodicea, A.D. 343-381. The council decreed that only specially appointed singers, usually choirs of monks, could present music sung in Latin.

The Reformation made great changes. Martin Luther capitalized on German interest in singing. Holding that music ranked next to theology, he exalted the role of congregational singing as well as the use of choirs. He wrote hymns which taught doctrine, and would rehearse new hymns during the week with the congregation. Not only did he write his hymns in the language of the people, but he adapted popular tunes sung in the beer gardens, thus setting all Germany singing Gospel truth in the garb of secular songs.

John Calvin permitted only psalms as suitable texts for

congregational singing. The influence of the psalter became a part of the Reformation in its sweep across Europe and England. The sole musical leadership was the "precentor," who announced the psalm, set the pitch, then "lined it out" phrase by phrase for the congregation to repeat.

Around 1700 Isaac Watts began writing church songs, such as "When I Survey the Wondrous Cross." He also gave a New Testament flavor to many psalms. "Jesus Shall Reign Where'er the Sun" is his version of Psalm 72. Altogether he penned 600 hymns, many of which are still favorites today.

The major contribution of the United States to hymnology is the Gospel song, which grew mainly out of camp meetings and Sunday Schools, and was later popularized in the Moody-Sankey evangelistic campaigns. Evangelical churches have continued to stress subjective songs, perhaps failing to achieve a good balance with objective hymns. As a result, sometimes a considerable gap exists between the material sung and the theology preached.

Since 1965 many evangelicals have experienced a mushrooming of new music. New sounds have flooded the churches with folksongs, guitars, tape tracks, and musicals for all ages. Many of these new songs express praise and adoration. One type is a repeated chorus with variations, the best known of which is "Alleluia." Another type is a Bible verse or portion set to music.

Resistance to New Music

The history of church music has always involved a conflict between the old and the new. New developments are usually regarded with suspicion by the traditionalist. For centuries church music was monophonic—all voices singing in unison and a single melody. When polyphony (harmony singing) was introduced, suspicious churches banned all "seductive and impure melodies."

In his encouragement of church music, Martin Luther stood virtually alone. John Calvin discouraged anything except the singing of psalms, recommending that songs have

only one note per syllable. Some Reformers went so far as to
raid churches and destroy some of Europe's grand organs,
arguing that they hindered true worship.

The first English Baptists had no music whatever. Later,
music was limited to psalm-singing by the congregation,
though many doubted the practice was according to the
mind of Christ, claiming that melody was to be made in the
heart, not publicly.

When Handel's *Messiah* first came out, it took a few years
to find acceptance among critics, who judged the music
shockingly secular and irreverent. We forget that all the
good old songs, now our favorites, were once new songs.

Few 19th-century churches permitted the use of pianos in
their services. Song-leader Charles Alexander used two
grand pianos in large auditoriums to assist his spontaneous
choral and congregational singing. His introduction of the
instrument in worship services sanctified the piano for
church use.

The Gospel songs of Moody's campaigns were criticized as
cheap, tawdry, and more suited to the dance hall than the
church. They had forgotten that the tune of "O Day of Rest
and Gladness," already in use in their churches, was heard
(and still is) in the beer gardens of Germany.

We should not be too quick to reject others' musical
choices. The music of primitive people offered in love is as
acceptable to God as Haydn's *Creation* or Handel's *Messiah*,
sung by large choirs with full orchestras. Musical offerings
should not be rejected just because they emanate from other
cultural sources or don't suit our personal preferences.

Prelude

The prelude should prepare individuals for worship. It is not
warm-up music which begins 10 minutes before the service,
nor is it merely cover-up music to drown out conversation,
though it may have a quieting effect. The prelude should
draw the worshipers' minds from mundane affairs to the
holy awe of God's presence.

Does non-hymn music have a place in a worship service? On the one hand, some believe that if the music has unfamiliar lyrics (or no lyrics at all) then the congregation won't get anything out of it.

On the other hand, who can fail to be moved by the instrumental "Pastoral Symphony" in the *Messiah?* In his essay "On Church Music," C. S. Lewis writes that "an excellently performed piece of music, as a natural operation which reveals in a very high degree the peculiar powers given to man, will thus always glorify God whatever the intention of the performers may be" (*Christian Reflections,* Eerdmans, p. 98).

Hymns

Hymns are used at several points in worship. The eight most common types of hymns are: (1) hymns of praise; (2) hymns of pardon (confession); (3) hymns of preparation (before Scripture reading or sermon); (4) hymns of petition (before or after prayer); (5) hymns of proffer (before or after offering); (6) hymns of purpose (dedication after sermon); (7) hymns of passion (for communion—often the *Sanctus*); and (8) hymns of parting (in connection with the benediction).

In a worship service, the first hymn should be a burst of praise, extolling the excellencies of the Triune God. Some churches begin with the "Doxology." Many do not realize that the traditional "Doxology" is really the last verse of a hymn, probably sung by more English-speaking Christians than any other stanza in existence. Many advocate its occasional use, feeling that overusage dilutes its freshness.

The "Gloria Patri" was used from the earliest days of the church. The last part, "As it was in the beginning, is now and ever shall be, world without end," was added after the Council of Nicea (A.D. 325) had made a strong statement concerning the Trinity. The "it" refers to the Trinity as existing from all eternity past. Thus it is appropriate to sing the "Gloria Patri" after reciting either the Apostles' or Nicean Creed. Or it could be repeated after the reading of Scripture.

Difference between Hymns and Spiritual Songs

Paul spoke of "psalms and hymns and spiritual songs" with which we should make melody to the Lord (Eph. 5:19; Col. 3:16).

Psalms. The *Psalter* was the chief hymnbook of the church for the first 1500 years. Martin Luther's great hymn, "A Mighty Fortress Is Our God," was created out of Psalm 46. Many of Isaac Watts' hymns were inspired by the psalms, but flavored with New Testament interpretation. There seems to be a revived interest today in putting psalms to music.

Hymns. What is a hymn? Augustine said it is a song of praise to God. This definition involves three elements: praise, praise of God, and publicly sung praise. The hymn must have definite motion Godward as it offers up the sacrifice of united, common worship.

Gospel Song. How does a hymn differ from a Gospel song? A hymn is the praise of God. A Gospel song is a testimony to people. A hymn expresses the worshiper's attitude toward God and focuses on God's attributes. A Gospel song is chiefly evangelistic, composed for use in large, mixed gatherings. It is usually subjective, concerning itself with the individual's salvation.

Hymns usually do not have a chorus, but most Gospel songs do. A hymn is literary in style, devotional in tone, and somewhat staid in tune. A Gospel song is more sentimental, with lyrics easily learned, and a catchy tune with lilting rhythm. Examples of Gospel songs are: "I Come to the Garden Alone," "Love Lifted Me," "Shall We Gather at the River?" and "When the Roll Is Called Up Yonder."

Selection of Hymns

Every believer can be involved in hymn-singing. Those who feel they cannot carry a tune should at least concentrate on the words. Special music—whether by choir, ensemble, or soloist—should not replace, but augment, congregational singing. A competent organist, assisted by a talented pianist, perhaps backed by an orchestra, all with enough volume to

carry the congregation along with them, will make for praiseful singing.

Unless you serve on a worship committee, you probably will have no responsibility for selecting hymns for Sunday morning worship. But if occasions arise to choose the hymns for smaller group services, here are some suggestions:

Know the difference between objective and subjective songs. In a worship service, the first hymn should be one of praise, adoration, or thanksgiving. The more intimate type is appropriate for the middle part, whereas closing hymns usually emphasize consecration and service.

Choose hymns with good literary style. Some hymns have survived despite mixed metaphors, doggerel, and poorly rhymed lines. Avoid the excessively vivid, vulgar, or repulsive. This stanza seems strange to modern ears:

> But get away, without delay,
> Christ pities not your cry;
> Depart to hell, there may you yell
> And roar eternally.

Robert S. Bridges, poet laureate of Great Britain from 1913-1930, was once asked permission to include one of his poems in a proposed collection of "the hundred best hymns." He gave permission, but added, "There are not 'a hundred best hymns' in the English language. There are not a hundred good ones." Though many of our hymns may not measure up to his high standard, it should not discourage the raising of our level of excellence.

Select hymns that are doctrinally sound. Is the substance biblical? Hymns should speak to the mind as well as to the emotions. Though many hymns tend to be more devotional than didactic, they should contain truth.

Choose hymns to fit the message or the theme of the service. After a sermon called "Launch Out Into the Deep," the congregation sang, "Pull for the Shore." After a message on hell, a soloist sang, "Tell Mother I'll Be There."

One minister pursued the course of singing the hymnbook right through consecutively. Seldom did a hymn meet the

need of the moment. Finally one Sunday morning when the parting hymn of benediction was sung in the middle of the service, the minister whispered to the organist, "From now on, you pick the hymns."

When asked what criterion a singer should use in selecting a Gospel song, George Beverly Shea replied, "The singer or choir director should know the subject of the pastor's message and stay on target with the minister, relying on the Holy Spirit to bless the sermon in song too." The proper wedding of song with sermon can intensify the impact of God's truth.

Choose hymns with appropriate music. The music should support and reinforce the words, not distract. Text and tune should produce unity of sound and message. Donald Hustad suggests fast tunes do not lend themselves to the spirit of devotional words, nor do slow tempos go well with enthusiastic testimony (*Jubilate!,* pp. 38-39). He gives examples of texts and music that are compatible: "The Solid Rock," "When I Survey the Wondrous Cross," and "O God, Our Help in Ages Past."

Hustad suggests that the music to "Love Lifted Me" is too rollicking and swingy for the tragic concept of "I was sinking deep in sin." Though the music for the stanza of "Alas and Did My Saviour Bleed?" is adequate, the spirited chorus between stanzas disrupts the worshiper's understanding of the extreme suffering endured by Christ on the cross. However, if the chorus is sung only once at the end, it fits the idea of the believer's joyful freedom from sin.

Favorite hymns can be sung to different well-known tunes. The metric index indicates that "From Greenland's Icy Mountains" can be sung to the melody of "Stand Up, Stand Up for Jesus," or that "Amazing Grace" fits the music of "Joy to the World."

Do not repeat the same hymns too often. Since the opening hymn should be one everybody knows, many churches repeat the same 30 hymns over and over. The average evangelical church uses less than 50 percent of its hymnbook.

To prevent such repetition, someone should maintain a record of hymns sung every Sunday. The person selecting the hymns should refer to this record so he won't repeat the same hymns too often.

Some churches try to learn a new hymn once a month. The organist includes it somewhere in the prelude, getting the congregation subconsciously familiar with it. The choir sings it through once, of course having practiced it previously. Just before the congregation tries it, the leader reads the text slowly as the organ plays the tune in the background. Even if the new hymn isn't sung as well as the favorites, the congregation probably pays more attention to the words in its struggle to master it, than if they were merely mouthing well-known words.

Avoid sentimentality. Often we overuse favorite songs, especially those deficient in poetry, theology, and musicality. When a song is chosen because of its delightful melody, words lose their importance. If the words are deemed unimportant, hymn-singing becomes a mere sentimental exercise. The problem has been compounded by commercialism in music publishing which caters to the evangelical "hit parade."

John Newton, converted six years after Handel composed the *Messiah,* came to admire this great oratorio. As a theologian and hymnwriter himself, Newton was concerned that the text of the *Messiah,* composed of about 76 Bible verses, be fully understood as people heard it sung. He asserted that to listen to the oratorio unresponsively was "no better than a profanation of the name and truths of God, a crucifying of the Son of God afresh."

Choirs

Though in some parts of the world today choirs are regarded as unessential or undesirable, American church life considers choirs important. In fact, the absence of an adult choir would be the most noticed event in a Sunday morning service, unless the pastor failed to appear.

Choirs provide music for church services, and give talented people opportunity to develop their abilities and to minister. A good choir, as well as a capable orchestra, can lead the congregation in strong hymn singing and can lift hearts to God through a quality of music beyond simple congregational singing.

The choir should be a model of decorum. Whispering voices or wandering inattention are irreverent. No choir member should leave before the sermon, unless in an emergency. Comfortable gowns add dignity, and by their uniformity remove the distraction of multi-colored dresses, suits, shirts, and ties.

Every church has a common range of music style on which the majority agree. Though most music will be selected from that spectrum, the worship leaders should occasionally choose more traditional or liturgical music, and at other times select more modern songs. Leaders may be accused, on the one hand, of using "highfalutin" music, or of going too contemporary. Evangelical churches should be open to broader experience in musical style.

The Duty of Praise

John Wesley gave these instructions for singing hymns. Learn the tunes. Sing them as printed. Sing lustily and with a good courage. Beware of singing as if you are half-dead, or half-asleep, but lift your voice with strength. Be no more afraid of your voice, nor more ashamed of its being heard, than when you sing the songs of Satan. Sing modestly. Do not bawl. Make one clear melodius sound. Sing in tune. Above all, sing spiritually. Attend strictly to the sense of what you sing, and see that your heart is not carried away with the sound, but offered to God continually.

We understand the enthusiasm of the preacher who exclaimed, "The three elements of public worship are preaching, prayer, and praise. The greatest of these is praise. For some day in heaven preaching and prayer will be done away with, but praise will still abide."

Let Us Pray

Two hundred years ago in America, the pastor's prayer usually lasted from 45 minutes to an hour. In Scotland a century ago, a prayer of 20 minutes was considered incomplete. Hourglasses were used in the service, not only to see that the minister kept within his alotted time, but also to make sure he did not shortchange parishioners through abbreviated prayers.

The concept of one long, comprehensive mid-service prayer wasn't the universal practice of the church. Justin Martyr described an early Christian worship service which contained two prayers after the sermon. At the Reformation period, Calvin's service had a minimum of three prayers. The habit of the "long" prayer seems not to have surfaced till the time of the Puritans in the 16th century.

One advantage of several shorter prayers is the lesser demand on the attention span of worshipers, thus helping to preserve their attitude of reverence. Another is clarity, since each prayer relates to a specific area. Several short prayers also help maintain a prayerful aura through the entire service. They progress from adoration to confession to intercession to dedication, with each prayer culminating at a higher level.

The pastor ministers as both prophet and priest. As prophet, he speaks for God to man. As priest, he speaks for men to God. Though every believer has the privilege of speaking to God directly for himself, in public prayer the pastor leads the entire congregation in acknowledging the excellencies of God, lifting up their needs, discerning His will, and dedicating themselves afresh to His service. To pray in a rambling, fumbling manner may lessen the nearness of God for those present. Without attempting to put on airs, the leader should direct the worshipers' thoughts Godward so that they can make the pastor's prayer their prayer.

Though the worshiper usually does none of the audible public praying, it will help his worship if he understands the rationale behind the various prayers in a regular service.

Invocation

The opening prayer is called the invocation. It is not primarily a prayer of praise, though it will likely contain a short reference to adoration. Neither is it a prayer of intercession, though it may make a simple petition. An invocation is a brief prayer inviting God's presence and power in the service so that the congregation may worship in a manner pleasing to Him.

If you are called on to offer an invocation, keep it short. To insure variety, familiarize yourself with the rich store of invocations in different denominational books of worship. Including scriptural thought in your prayer will bring vitality.

The Pastoral Prayer

As the minister becomes the voice of his congregation, worshipers are often reminded of their oneness with the people of God everywhere. Since the pastoral prayer is somewhat expanded, its component parts can be recalled by the acronym ACTS (Adoration, Confession, Thanksgiving, and Supplication).

Adoration. Most people are better at asking than adoring. We come more with petition than praise. One minister said,

"Too many Christians try to put all their begs in one askit." But in the first part of the pastoral prayer, we should reverently extol God for His majesty and grace.

Confession. Many liturgical churches provide for confession of sin soon after the invocation. For churches that don't, this is a good time for the minister to lead the congregation in acknowledging their transgressions and assuring their pardon through Christ's abounding grace.

Thanksgiving. How immature it is for us to beseech God for things while forgetting what He has already done for us. Yet it's much easier, though wrong, to think of what we need than of what we already have.

The "General Thanksgiving" in the *Book of Common Prayer* is a good example of a prayer of thanks:

> Almighty God, Father of all mercies, we, Thine unworthy servants, do give Thee most humble and hearty thanks for all Thy goodness and loving-kindness to us, and to all men. We bless Thee for our creation, preservation, and all the blessings of this life; but above all, for Thine inestimable love in the redemption of the world by our Lord Jesus Christ; for the means of grace, and for the hope of glory.

The prayer ends by asking that thankfulness may be expressed not only verbally, but by lives of service and righteousness.

Supplication (Petition). Petition is a prominent feature of prayer. The Lord's Prayer is mostly petition. Paul wrote, "I exhort . . . that . . . supplications, prayers, intercessions, and giving of thanks, be made for all men" (1 Tim. 2:1).

When petitioning God, the pastor should include requests representative of all kinds of people—youth, middle-aged, and elderly—for there will likely be one broken heart, whether lonely, sick, or sorrowing, in almost every pew.

"Bidding prayers" is an historic practice in which a topic for prayer is announced. With bowed heads, all are asked to pray silently, after which the minister voices a collective prayer. In modern practice, the "bidding prayer" can mean

the invitation to silent, then spoken prayer. Some churches encourage members to send up requests to be read at a specified time in the service.

Length of Pastoral Prayer
In recent years the length of the pastoral prayer has decreased. The prayer, if too curt and snappy, may seem irreverent. But if the prayer is too long, people may get fidgety.

D. L. Moody's practicality came to the fore during a series of meetings near London, England. A minister who had been asked to pray went on longer than the evangelist wished. In a firm but kind voice, Moody announced, "While the good brother is finishing his prayer, we will sing a hymn." Long prayers are for our private times with God; short prayers are for the pulpit.

Manner of Praying
Prayer is usually addressed to the Father, in the merits of the Son, and through the ministry of the Holy Spirit. Since the prayer is directed to God, the leader should not try to impress his hearers with linguistic mastery. Yet, because the leader is praying in the presence of people, he has some responsibilities in the manner of utterance.

Prayer should be reverent, fervent, and sincere. Mingled with boldness of approach, we need to come with a sense of awe before the throne of God. Though pleading may become urgent and impassioned, the voice should always be natural. A church member, trying to describe a deacon, exclaimed, "You know—the man who cries when he prays."

Prayer should contain clear, fresh, and varied language. Simple words are preferable. Too many people repeat the same phrases in every prayer. Constant, "We beseech Thee," or "Lord, give us," becomes monotonous. We should try to avoid the invoking of God at the start of every sentence, whether it's "Our heavenly Father," or "O Lord."

Prayer should be specific, definite enough to reach the heart, but not too personal or embarrassing. We should not

just pray, "Bless our children," but "Watch over our children that they may be diligent in their school studies."

Those who pray publicly should have in mind the struggles, victories, defeats, sorrows, joys, fears, and hopes of those present. Leaders should cultivate detail without triviality. A minister at prayer meeting, after having a new set of false teeth put in, was quite amused when one good brother prayed pointedly, "Lord, we thank Thee that Thou hast given our dear pastor new artificial members. Bless them to the proclamation of Thy truth."

Prayer should not indulge in personalities nor scolding. A person should never take a crack at someone who irks him, using prayer. Some preachers feel safer admonishing their people through prayer than through preaching. Perhaps they think that somehow in prayer they have God on their side. But prayer should not be a subtle sermon.

Prayer should not include announcements. Suddenly in the midst of his prayer, a minister asked God to comfort a mother who had just returned from the bedside of her dying son. A rustle swept over the crowd. No longer were hearts intent on prayer, but rather curious about identities and details. Not until the Amen sounded and the name of the youth was announced did the people calm down. Such announcements should be made before prayer.

We should not give information in prayer, like the college president closing a chapel service who suddenly realized he had omitted an announcement. He inserted in the benediction this message, "O Lord, bless the French class which Thou knowest will not meet at the usual hour, but at 10:45 this morning."

Pastoral prayers should have progression. Already one suggested order has been given acrostically, ACTS—adoration, confession, thanksgiving, and supplication.

Petitions should follow in some logical sequence. For example, requests could proceed from the needs of the individual, to the church, to the community, to the nation, to the world. Or, beginning the prayer with adoration, it could also

end with adoration. This progression is seen in the Lord's Prayer, which begins with "Thy kingdom come," and ends with "Thine is the kingdom."

Prayer should be given some advance thought. If for a 30-minute sermon a preacher studies for 10 hours, doesn't it seem logical that for a 5-minute prayer he should prepare too?

Someone objects, "Isn't the spirit of prayer more important than the technique of prayer? It's a matter of the heart." But public prayer is a matter of *many* hearts! Unprepared prayer may dance and skip and lead nowhere.

The leader should jot down the various items for prayer—classifying them under adoration, confession, thanksgiving, and supplication. This would reveal an over-emphasis of any area, thus achieving an overall balance.

To help in public prayer, we should be acquainted with the language of Scripture. Our Puritan forefathers wanted to free us from total reliance on written, formal prayers so we could pray more specifically. But they were steeped in the Bible. They lived, breathed, and prayed by the Book. Today, by not being so securely linked to the Bible, we have let our prayers degenerate into hackneyed, meandering clichés.

Prayer for Illumination

The prayer for illumination is a simple petition for divine enlightenment on the reading or preaching of God's truth. The prayer might be as brief as this: "May the Holy Spirit shed His sacred light upon the holy page. Amen."

Prayer of Dedication

The minister may wish to offer a prayer after the sermon to help the congregation respond to its spiritual impact, and to vow some new intent for their lives. The members of the congregation should be led in a prayer asking God to shape their hearts after the image of Christ so that they may glorify God in their homes, businesses, neighborhoods, and churches.

Collects

The normal pattern of many liturgies calls for a period of prayer petition after the sermon, sometimes in conjunction with the prayer of dedication. Some liturgical churches use prayers called "collects" at this time. By the fourth century, liturgies had collects for every Sunday in the year. Coming from the Latin "collecta," the word originally meant a prayer offered as believers were collecting or assembling. Then it came to signify the gathering together of the prayers of the congregation by the pastor as he offered them to God as one prayer.

Collects, remarkable for their conciseness, follow a definite structure, embodying five different parts in one sentence: address to God, relative clause with attribute or description of God, petition, purpose of plea, and conclusion or doxology. These compact and vigorous compositions compel attention. Here's an example, the collect for the first Sunday in Lent:

O Lord, who for our sake didst fast 40 days and 40 nights; give us grace to use such abstinence, that, our flesh being subdued to the Spirit, we may ever obey Thy godly motions in righteousness, and true holiness, to Thy honor and glory, who livest and reignest with the Father and the Holy Ghost, one God, world without end. Amen.

Collects aimed to gather up the inward desires of worshipers, formalize them in compact and explicit utterance, and offer them as a united petition to God. A minister often read an entire series of collects, for they were written for a whole range of spiritual needs.

Benediction

The prayer of benediction seeks God's continuing providence, power, and presence to follow the members of the congregation as they leave for the outside world. The most commonly used church benediction was written by Paul: "The grace of the Lord Jesus Christ, and the love of God, and

the communion of the Holy Ghost, be with you all. Amen."
(2 Cor. 13:14). Sometimes the Aaronic blessing is used (Num.
6:24-26) or the benediction from Hebrews 13:20-21.

Usually the pastor raises his arm as he begins the benediction, which may or may not be followed by a choral or congregational response. After the benediction and response, the congregation should remain in a posture of reverence until the signal for dismissal is given.

Amen

Saying Amen after a prayer is both an Old and New Testament practice. The rabbis said that uttering an Amen was like adding your name to an epistle written by another. The congregation's Amen was part of the Corinthian church's service (1 Cor. 14:16).

Perhaps ministers should educate their people to say a hearty but reverent Amen at the end of the pastoral prayer. In reality, it may be out of place for the minister alone to say the Amen, since an Amen is an endorsement by others to what has been prayed. It's the people's *So be it* in assent to the pastor's prayer.

The Early Church Prayed Together

When Peter and John were released from prison, they went immediately to their own group to report what had happened. In response, the believers all "lifted up their voices to God with one accord" (Acts 4:24). How did the entire assembly join in this prayer? Was it by saying Amen throughout or at the end? Was it by repeating the words after the person who prayed them aloud? Was it by reciting together the part of Psalm 2 quoted in the prayer?

In any event, the prayer was answered, for the place was shaken. The believers were filled with the Holy Ghost, spoke the Word of God with boldness, shared their goods with the needy, and gave a powerful witness of the Resurrection.

When the church of the 20th century prays worshipfully, we too will see the Lord work in a wonderful way.

Let Us Open Our Bibles

A newly converted boy was deeply distressed. He approached a missionary and said, "My big watchdog just tore a page out of my New Testament and swallowed it!"

The missionary tried to comfort him, "We can get another New Testament. Don't worry."

But the boy would not be consoled. So the missionary said, "If your dog can crunch an ox bone, he isn't going to be hurt by swallowing a piece of paper."

"Oh," cried the boy, "I was once very bad. If I had an enemy, I hated him, and everything in me wanted to kill him. But when I got the New Testament in my heart, I began to love everybody and forgive my enemies. Now my big hunting dog has got the Book in him, and he'll start to love the lions, and let them help themselves to my sheep and oxen!"

This boy knew that feeding on God's Word affects our behavior. Undoubtedly this is one reason Scripture reading has always had a vital part in Christian worship services through the centuries.

Since worship involves our response to God's revelation, we must first become acquainted with the divine revelation in order to properly respond. The infallible source of God's message for us is the Bible, which tells us how we may be

redeemed through the work of Jesus Christ. Forgiveness of sins elicits the reaction of our praise. Then the Bible outlines man's duty as a believer. The response of obedience in everyday life is in itself a form of worship. S. S. Curry in *Vocal and Literary Interpretation of the Bible* says, "Bible reading was the most important element in the worship of the early church" (Expression Co., Boston, p. IX).

Survey of Public Scripture Reading

Moses read the Book of the Covenant to all the people (Deut. 29). On leading the Israelites into Canaan, Joshua read to them "all the words of the Law, the blessings and cursings" (Josh. 8:34). The Book of the Law, recovered when the temple was repaired in the reign of King Josiah, the king himself read in the ears of "all the people, great and small" (2 Chron. 34:30).

The regular public reading of the Law originated with the synagogue during the Babylonian captivity. From a pulpit of wood during the Feast of Tabernacles, Ezra read the scroll of the Law of Moses to the returned exiles. When he unrolled it, the congregation stood up, answered Amen, lifted up hands, bowed heads, and worshiped God. For six hours the expectant multitude remained standing, "attentive unto the Book of the Law" (Neh. 8:1-6).

The synagogue service consisted largely of the reading of the Scripture. Even today the Jewish synagogue has as its focal point the ark containing the sacred scrolls. One day Jesus read the Scripture lesson in His hometown synagogue at Nazareth. He added excitement to the event by claiming the Scriptures were fulfilled in their ears. No wonder all eyes were fastened on Him (Luke 4:20).

In the early church, witnesses would recount some wonder Jesus had performed, or some sermon He had given. Oral reports of His miracles and parables would be written down and circulated among early gatherings. The inspired accounts that later emerged were the books of Matthew, Mark, Luke, and John. Following the model of Jesus Himself, Peter,

and Paul, teachers would show how Jesus fulfilled Old Testament Scripture (Luke 24:25-27, 44-48; Acts 2:16-41, 3:18; 17:1-3).

Paul wrote the Colossians, "And when this epistle is read among you, cause that it be read also in the church of the Laodiceans" (4:16). Paul told Timothy to give attention "to reading, to exhortation, to doctrine" (1 Tim. 4:13), which were public reading of Scriptures, preaching and teaching. Peter referred to Paul's epistles, which had probably been read formally in the churches (2 Peter 3:15-16). In the salutation of Revelation, John invoked a blessing on both those who read aloud his book, and the assembled congregation who heard and kept what was enjoined (1:3).

Often through history the reading of Scripture was a powerful instrument in religious awakenings. It was so when Savonarola read from his little Bible before thousands in Florence. Martin Luther's Bible awoke the conscience of Germany.

The Bible is not read in any systematic manner in most Protestant churches today. A survey within a large denomination indicated that 20 percent of the churches read no Scripture on Sunday morning. Another 30 percent said that the only Scripture read on most Sunday mornings came from the Gospels. Surprisingly, in some evangelical churches Bible reading is a scarce commodity. This stems from the heritage of revivalism in which the preacher simply took a text, or read a brief passage, and then delivered a long sermon on it.

Churches should arrange their order of service to include an ample reading of Scripture. After all, the Bible is the Word of God, possessing superior authority over the sermon. Its repeated reading in worship testifies to the historical origin of our faith, centered in the revelation of God in Jesus Christ, predicted and foreshadowed in the Law and the Prophets, fulfilled in the Gospels, amplified in the Epistles, and culminated in the Book of Revelation.

Many churches have lay-readers who from time to time

read the Scripture in the public services. Many of us are called on to read a Bible portion in smaller meetings. Perhaps the following suggestions may prove helpful.

Read Well

For many, Scripture-reading is yawn time, or an occasion to read the bulletin. Perhaps the Bible falls on deaf ears because of poor reading. Stumbling over difficult passages and mispronouncing words hinder worship. The rubric in the *Book of Common Prayer* directs the reader to turn himself so as to be best heard, and to read distinctly with an audible voice.

A reader should go over the passage in advance, so as to read with clarity, expression, and accuracy. Since good reading is often a matter of proper understanding, the reader should know the setting and meaning of the Scripture. He should convey the impression that what he is reading is of great importance, not that he is reading just because the order of service calls for it.

Read with Reverence

The Bible was written by holy men inspired by the Holy Ghost, deals with holy subjects, and should help us live holy lives. The "holy" Bible should receive reverent handling.

In the Church of Scotland the sexton solemnly carries the Bible in at the start of the service, places it on the pulpit, as the congregation stands in silence. Some churches have the Bible brought in by a child, or teenager, or deacon, when the leaders and choir have reached their places. In earlier years in New England, the people stood for the reading of the Bible. Also, it was common to leave an open Bible on the Lord's table at all times. Such gestures picture visibly the central position the Bible occupies in our thinking.

Read All Parts of the Bible

Scholars think that the synagogue service had readings from the Law and the Prophets which covered most of the Old

Testament every three years. The day Jesus read the Scripture in His hometown synagogue, He was likely reading the lesson from Isaiah 61. But many evangelical churches today have no systematic plan to read the whole range of Scripture.

The pulpit Bible of a capable preacher had been placed in the pulpit as a new volume 25 years ago. Its pages told its tale of use, abuse, and no use. Almost the first half of the Bible remained as clean as the day it left the press. The pages of the Psalms and Isaiah had been turned over many times. So had the pages of the Gospels. But the Epistle to the Romans was almost worn through with constant use, and its eighth chapter was in holes.

Churches through the centuries have constructed lectionaries. This time-honored practice provides Old Testament, Epistle, and Gospel lessons for every Sunday of the year. Newer lectionaries have a three-year cycle that allows for the public reading of all four Gospels in their entirety, most of the Epistles, and a relevant portion of the Old Testament. The rationale for a lectionary is to hear as much of God's Word as possible over a given period, rather than the same familiar portions over and over again. Since continuous reading of Bible books is maintained with as little interruption as possible, preachers can align their sermons to the readings and preach in-depth sermons from one book for several weeks.

Some argue that the consecutive reading of Scripture breaks up the unity of a service by making it impossible to have one theme around which songs, Scripture, and sermon can be built. But is a unified service important enough to forego reading the complete sweep of scriptural content? A competent minister of music can weave hymns, anthems, and special numbers around both separate Scripture reading and sermon texts.

The Lord's people should hear the entire range of the Bible every few years. Too often only New Testament sections are read, depriving the congregation of the background

of God's dealing in earlier centuries. The reading of both Testaments demonstrates the unity of Scripture, and the relationship between the two covenants.

Use Variety

Scripture may be read in unison, responsively, by choric speech, or by leaders. Sometimes the Scripture can be sung by the choir when that particular passage has been made into an anthem. Sometimes a church has two readings of the same text, one from the *King James Version,* and the other from another version. Some have used the arts to reinforce the Word, such as pantomime, pictures, slides, or mini-drama.

The value of responsive reading has been questioned. Such readings do give another opportunity for all to participate, and thus bind the congregation together. Also antiphonal worship is scriptural. However, the psalms were written to be sung, not read. Also, group reading tends to break up the sense of the passage by focusing attention on stopping and starting.

Should Comment Be Added to the Scripture Reading?

Strange as it may seem, early New England churches virtually prohibited the reading of the Bible in their pulpits unless accompanied by comments. Unadorned reading reminded them of the liturgy which they had fled. On the other hand, some say that we should let the pure Word of God speak for itself.

The location of the passage should always be given by book, chapter, and verse. It should be announced clearly twice so that none may miss it. Members should be encouraged to bring and follow along in their own Bibles, even though pew Bibles may be provided.

But more elucidation may be in order. Having studied the passage in advance, the reader may give a brief word of introduction, telling why this particular section was chosen, or setting it in its context.

If reading from the *King James Version,* it might be helpful for the reader to point out when a word has changed its meaning. For example, the word *conversation* in the 17th century never meant "speech," but "manner of life." Paraphrasing, substituting, or summarizing all help people better understand difficult passages.

It has been my practice in over three decades in the pastorate to read the Bible through consecutively chapter by chapter and make comments on the chapter I read each week. Of course, the danger always exists of letting the comment grow into a sermonette. But if a person has the ability to condense the gist of a passage into a few short sentences, or to enlighten its essence by some pithy remark, he should use his gift. Those who heard Spurgeon's comment on the Scripture reading said such exposition was often superior to his sermon. He himself said that as a rule he spent more time on the Bible reading preparation than on the sermon.

Creeds

Creeds were first formulated to teach Bible truths liturgically. No formal creed (fixed confession embodying the Bible's fundamental doctrines) is found in the New Testament. But there are repeated references to a collection of distinctive beliefs, once for all delivered to the saints and held fast as a sacred deposit from God, especially in the face of heretical attacks. Some terms for this body of truth are "the apostles' doctrine" (Acts 2:42); "that form of doctrine" (Rom. 6:17); "this rule" (Gal. 6:16); "the Word of life" (Phil. 2:16); "the words of faith and of good doctrine" (1 Tim. 4:6); and "the form of sound words" (2 Tim. 1:13). This deposit of faith was the basis of acceptance into the Christian community, the ground on which excommunication was to be exercised, and the message which was to be handed on to succeeding generations (2 Tim. 2:2).

Though perhaps first expressed in simple sentences like "Jesus is Lord," or "Jesus is the Christ," this deposit of faith seems to have been expressed as a creedal formula in Paul's

first letter to the Corinthians. The fourfold "that" introduces each part of the creed (15:3-5). The four elements of the creed were:

that Christ died for our sins according to the Scriptures (v. 3)

that he was buried (v. 4)

that He rose again the third day according to the Scriptures (v. 4)

that He was seen of Cephas, then of the Twelve (v. 5)

Though many disdain the use of a creed in a church service as a mindless reciting of words, such confessions of faith seem to have scriptural basis. First Timothy 3:16 seems to be a clear example of an early formula in which the church gave expression to the fundamental facts of the Gospel. The *King James Version* begins, "without controversy," which is better translated, "admittedly," or "confessedly," and which the *Revised Standard Version* renders, "we confess." Then follows a series of statements which trace the career of the Lord Jesus from His preexistence, through His incarnate life on earth, His resurrection, and His ascension into the Father's presence.

Many churches use the Apostle's Creed or the Nicene Creed in their services. It might be profitable for nonliturgical churches to occasionally include one of these creeds in their order of service.

Creeds help give us a sense of heritage. They also enable us to affirm our faith. They serve as a means of praise to God. They grant a sense of unity with believers worldwide, who also affirm the same faith.

Sermon and Supper

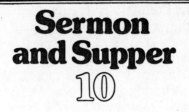

10

The sermon has a notable heritage, going back to synagogue worship where, after the reading of the Law in Hebrew and Aramaic paraphrases of the Law known as Targums, came the delivery of a sermon. Being asked to read the Scripture in the synagogue services provided Paul with his opportunity to evangelize the Jews on his missionary journeys (Acts 13:46ff; 17:1-3).

Before the Reformation the level of preaching was very low—mainly an illiterate clergy addressing a less literate congregation. Exposition of Scripture was not common; theology was neglected. Short homilies were often drawn from books which contained a collection of homilies, known as "Sleepwells" because they enabled inadequate preachers to get a peaceful sleep on Saturday nights. The most famous of these books was titled *Dormi Secure* (Sleep Without Care).

In our day the sermon has fallen into disrepute in many places. It has been called one of the great hardships inflicted on mankind, a sort of dagger in the back which could possibly deal a deathblow to Protestantism. Some have gone so far as to advocate a moratorium on preaching. The sermon may be in trouble because of its content, or because of its delivery. All that is spoken over the pulpit Sunday mornings

is not biblical preaching. Some is merely commentary on current events, or group therapy to assuage fears and allay frustrations. True preaching expounds the Word of God and applies it to everyday life.

Even when Bible exposition is given, it's not always presented interestingly. The pastor may not have prepared carefully to present a fresh, enlightening interpretation of the text. Certainly a sermon, to be immortal, need not be eternal. Twenty-five minutes would probably be the length of the average Sunday morning sermon, though some churches may feature 45-minute messages. Usually, the longer the sermon, the shorter the impact. Strangely, the good sermon is usually regarded as too short, and the poor one as too long.

How to Listen to a Sermon

Attitude is most important. The parishioner must approach the moment of the sermon with eager anticipation. He must believe the Lord is going to speak to him about some vital teaching or duty.

A man who attended the morning service, but never the evening service, was asked why. He replied, "I simply cannot digest more than one sermon a day." His questioner retorted, "I rather think the fault is not with your digestion, but with your appetite."

Eyes should be kept open. A man fell asleep while the preacher was delivering a message on eternal punishment. Toward the close the preacher shouted, "Those who want to go to a lost eternity, stand up." The man heard "stand up" and did so. He gazed around, and with a perplexed look on his face, said, "Preacher, I don't know what we're voting on, but it looks like you and I are the only ones for it."

Some decades ago in the Netherlands some sermons were preached in two parts. A song was inserted after the first half to keep the person in the pew from falling asleep, or to wake him, if snoozing. Another liturgical technique authorized the custodian to use a long pole to administer a sharp rap on the head of any sleeper.

Psychology says that when the eyes are closed, hearing becomes more acute. People can be seen making this experiment in most church services. But too often the experiment works the other way—with closed eyes leading to drowsiness.

Every effort should be made to learn what the sermon is about. The listener should open his Bible to the text, and keep it open during the message, noting the preacher's main points. The better prepared the sermon, the easier it is to follow. Many churches place a sheet in each Sunday bulletin headed "Sermon Notes," with space for the listener to record the main points, subpoints, and personal application.

The listener should probe his own heart to determine what action the sermon calls for. Often a congregation is encouraged to respond to the sermon in some appropriate way— whether in renewing some forgotten vow, making some new resolution (like tithing), setting up a devotional period each day, seeking forgiveness of some person wronged, or visiting a deprived person.

A responsive audience does much to create an atmosphere for warm worship. As each hearer opens his heart, the speaker senses his response, and is encouraged. Eloquence is due not only to an eloquent speaker but to eloquent hearers. Also, as each listener welcomes the message, he senses his neighbor's faith responding too. Thus the fire will spread from heart to heart.

The Relation of the Sermon to Other Parts

Many worship experts suggest that services should usually be built around one major theme, that of the sermon. If the pastor could let the minister of music review his sermons three or four weeks in advance, this would permit the selection and practice by musical participants of fitting numbers. If the sermon could not be completed that far in advance, then a general outline of the message would be helpful to the music people.

Some leaders believe that the elements of a service need

not be built around one theme, but can stand by themselves. The Holy Spirit may choose to speak through unrelated components, leaving the leader and congregation open to the workings of the Spirit.

An example of blending various parts with the sermon took place in a church in Pasadena, California. In connection with a message on the Second Coming of Christ, and just before the choir was to sing about Christ's return, the pastor had two laymen read recent newspaper headlines, one after another, for about 60 seconds, giving items that seemed to indicate imminent fulfillment of prophecies.

Another way to emphasize the points in a sermon is to sing a fitting hymn after each major point. This provides better concentration as well as drives home the salient thoughts of the message. A man reported seeing Dr. Richard Halverson, when pastor of the Fourth Presbyterian Church in Washington, sit down after preaching half the sermon. Then the congregation stood and sang awhile. Then the worshipers sat down and Dr. Halverson finished his sermon.

The Word Visualized—The Lord's Supper

Preaching presents Christ to the ears; the Lord's Supper presents Christ to the eyes. Communion is as much declaration as oral preaching. Augustine defined preaching as an audible sacrament, and sacraments as acted-out sermons.

Distortions of the apostolic Lord's Supper developed in early centuries. The pastor became a priest who by his official power was able to change the bread and wine into the very body and blood of Christ, and to repeatedly offer this sacrifice for the forgiveness of sins. Instead of sharing in the elements as in the first century, believers came as spectators to witness the offering of this sacrifice, and even to worship the elevated bread as the divine host. The aura of dread revolving around this veneration deterred worshipers from taking communion. Before long, most believers were participating only once a year, their minimum obligation. At the same time the sermon suffered by reduction or omission.

The Reformers set out to correct this situation. They reinstated preaching to its apostolic prominence. They also aimed to restore the Lord's Supper to its primitive simplicity and importance. John Calvin is sometimes cited as wishing to replace Communion with a preaching service. Though he did wish to have the Scripture read and expounded through a sermon in every service, he also wished to celebrate the Lord's Supper every week. But the city fathers would not permit him to do so. He had to settle for once a month. But to help people observe it more frequently, he suggested churches have it on different Sundays of the month so people could take it more often.

God's message and God's drama are not to be separated. Through baptism and the Lord's Supper the truth of the Word is reinforced. Calvin saw the two ordinances as taking the place of miracles, visions, and special phenomena God used in Old Testament times. Since baptism is initiatory, and not repeatable, we'll deal only with Communion. Sermon and Supper provide the basic means of publishing the Gospel. Whereas Catholicism has magnified the Supper over the sermon, Protestantism has often exalted the sermon over the Supper. Many churches err in making Communion an appendage to a service instead of a major opportunity for worship in its own right.

Communion goes by several other names: breaking of bread, Lord's Table, Lord's Supper, bread and cup, and Eucharist, which simply means "thanks." It was instituted by Christ, commanded by Christ, recommissioned by Paul, and practiced by the early church. Sadly, Christians have disagreed on their views on Communion. The four major viewpoints are: Catholic, Lutheran, Reformed, and Symbolic.

The Catholic view holds to transubstantiation, which means that the bread and wine are changed in their substance into the body and blood of Christ, to become each time a renewed sacrifice of Christ through which forgiveness is granted to those participating in the Mass.

The Lutheran view does not believe in such a changeover

of substance, but does hold that the body and blood of Christ are present along with the bread and wine. This opinion is termed consubstantiation, though some Lutherans would reject this terminology as philosophically inappropriate. But in some mysterious way Christ is present in the Lord's Supper.

The Reformed view denies any physical presence of Christ in the Communion, but believes in His dynamic presence. As the sun, though in the heavens, makes its light and heat to be present on earth, so the body of Christ, though in heaven, radiates an influence received by believers at the Lord's Table. Calvin held that there was something supernatural, miraculous, but also inexplicable in this divine ordinance.

The Symbolic view, sometimes called the *Memorialist,* insists that the bread and wine remain simply bread and wine. Those who hold this view deny that the Lord's Supper is an occasion for special grace from God. Rather, they affirm that the value of Communion rests in the believers' remembrance of Christ's sacrifice on the cross. Through that remembrance believers recognize their reliance on Christ for salvation and renew their dedication to Him.

This view holds that when Jesus said, "This is My body" (Luke 22:19), He was using a figure of speech just as He did when He said, "I am the door" (John 10:9). Christ was not a door with hinges and knob; neither was that bread and wine His actual body and blood. Symbolists acknowledge the Lord's presence in the Communion service to the same extent He is present in the rest of the service in fulfillment of His promise to be where two or three are gathered in His name (Matt. 18:20).

All agree blessings come with the Lord's Supper, if not from it. The blessings come from looking in many directions.

Backward. The bread and wine cause us to look back to the cross where Jesus' body was broken and His blood shed for us. We partake of these elements in remembrance of Him. There His sacrifice made possible our forgiveness and restoration to God's family. Not only do we remember His death, but we proclaim it as well (1 Cor. 11:26).

Upward. We lift our hearts heavenward to thank God for His abounding grace expressed through Christ's great sacrifice. We renew our faith in His finished work, which includes His resurrection for our justification and His ascension to the right hand of the Father for our intercession. By partaking of the bread and wine, we symbolize our continued appropriation of the benefits of His redemption.

Outward. Fellowship at the Lord's Table has a horizontal effect. Not only are we joined with an unseen Master, we are also knit with His people. Participation in a single loaf symbolizes our oneness in the body of Christ (1 Cor. 10:17).

In the early church it was customary to have a love feast before the observance of the Lord's Supper. But inconsistently some believers formed themselves into cliques, with the result that the poor were deprived of food and were hungry, whereas the well-to-do became surfeited and drunken through their abundance which they failed to share with the poor. Paul warned that failure to discern the unity of the Lord's body could result in sickness and even death (11:29-30). Today, many churches take a special offering at the Communion service to alleviate the needs of the poor, orphans, widows, sick, strangers, and prisoners.

Many descriptions of the ancient Communion service refer to the practice of the holy kiss, observed before the taking of the elements. This ritual encouraged unity among the body, for it would have been difficult for believers to embrace when not in agreement with each other.

Inward. Introspection has its place prior to the Lord's Table. Paul spoke about judging ourselves, so as not to be judged by the Lord (vv. 31-32). In New Zealand, a bushman in the first row of a church walked to the front where he knelt to receive the Communion bread. But a few seconds later, before partaking, he stood up and returned to his seat. Questioned later, he explained, "I did not know whom I would be kneeling beside. Suddenly I saw next to me a man who a few years ago killed my father and drank his blood, and whom I had vowed I would some day kill. Imagine how I felt when I

found him beside me. A rush of emotion swept over me, and I just couldn't partake of the bread, so I went back to my seat. Then I recalled Jesus' words, 'By this shall all men know that ye are My disciples, if ye have love one to another' (John 13:35). That overpowered me, and I went forward again. As I did, I recalled another verse, which Jesus spoke on the cross, 'Father, forgive them, for they know not what they do' (Luke 23:34). Then I was able to take the bread."

We need not be perfect to participate. No Christian should stay away from the Table because of any feeling of personal unworthiness, as long as he is trusting Christ and aims to obey Him. No one is really worthy. We honor *His* worth.

Forward. Paul wrote that believers were to observe this ordinance till Christ comes back (1 Cor. 11:26). How contradictory it is for us to take the Lord's Supper and not believe in the Second Coming of Christ—for at the Marriage Supper of the Lamb, Christ will sit down with His bride, the church. Anticipating the fulfillment of this hope gives great joy.

Conduct of the Communion Service

A minimal observance would include at least the following actions: a word of institution, often that given by the Apostle Paul (1 Cor. 11:23-26); a prayer of consecration for the bread, either by pastor or layman; the breaking of a piece of bread followed by the giving of the plates of bread to the deacons, one of whom will serve the pastor; the distribution of the bread to the congregation; the serving of the deacons by the pastor; and the invitation to all to "take, eat." After moments of meditation, the prayer is offered for the cup which is distributed in the same manner as the bread. When all have been served, the pastor says, "Drink, all of you." Again, after moments of silence, a hymn of praise is sung. A benediction may be pronounced or in some churches these words are given, "And when they had sung an hymn, they went out" (Matt. 26:30).

Some churches have the congregation come up front for the bread and cup, row by row, receiving the elements from

the minister or deacons. Many churches use unleavened bread, previously broken into small pieces, and grape juice. Some churches use a large loaf from which each participant breaks a piece, as it is passed to him. Sometimes a common cup is passed from person to person along with a cloth which is used for wiping before each sip.

In some churches, as a member passes the elements to the next person, he repeats, "Christ's body was broken for you," or "Christ's blood was shed for you." Sometimes special choir numbers may be sung during the distribution of the elements, or the organ may play familiar hymns of the Cross.

Frequency

The New Testament never gave instructions as to how often the Lord's Supper should be observed. Some modern denominations have it quarterly. Others observe it every other week, alternating between emphasis on sermon and Supper. Many churches have it once a month, usually on the first Sunday. Some churches alternate their monthly Communion service between morning and evening services.

In preparation for this book, I asked some 40 Christian leaders about their most memorable worship experiences. Approximately half of them said that the most unforgettable worship event was a Communion service overseas in which they joined with believers from other cultures. Several wrote of the impact of the Communion service at the 1976 International Congress on World Evangelism in Lausanne, Switzerland where 4,000 worshipers from dozens of nations took part. Perhaps such experiences move us deeply because they are a foretaste of that day when people from every tongue and nation will gather around the resurrected Lamb to sing His praises.

And Now—
The Offering
11

Three tightwads, visiting a church for the first time, went late to avoid the offering. To their dismay, this church took up the offering *after* the sermon. When the offering was announced, one fainted and the other two carried him out.

To place the offering at the end of the service may be surprising, but many liturgical orders of worship call for the offering after the sermon. After God speaks to the worshipers through the Scripture and sermon, they then give a tangible response to Him.

Whether taken at the beginning, middle, or end of the service, the offering is an act of worship. Money is personality in coin, representing the brawn and brain of the person who earned it. Thus, giving is a recognition of our deep devotion to our Lord for all He is and does. In fact, the amount given in relation to our total income may be a good indicator of our love for God. Through the offering, love in abstract becomes worship in concrete.

The offering should be regarded as a high point in the worship hour. From earliest times sacrifice has been the central act of worship. Cain and Abel brought offerings, though Cain's was unacceptable (Gen. 4:2-5). Noah, on emerging from the ark, brought sacrifices (8:20-22). Abra-

ham brought tithes to Melchizedek (14:18-20). The Levitical system required the giving of tithes as part of worship (Lev. 23:37-38). The Israelites brought gifts at the three major feasts each year, for the divine command said, "None shall appear before Me empty" (Ex. 23:15). Multitudes of sacrifices were presented at the dedication of Solomon's temple (1 Kings 8:62-66). Later, money put in Joash's chest was used to repair the temple (2 Kings 12:4-16). The wise men brought gifts in worship of the Christ Child (Matt. 2:11). The Bible says, "Honor the Lord with thy substance, and with the first-fruits of all thine increases" (Prov. 3:9).

Some pastors, to make the offering more meaningful, come down from the pulpit and hand the offering plates to the ushers. When the plates are brought back, the pastor receives them, then offers a prayer of dedication. For reasons of security some churches place the offering plates immediately in a vault. In such cases the offertory prayer should be made before the ushers take the offering.

An offertory prayer is not to scold the people for skimpy giving. Instead it should express thanks for God's abundant blessings, dedicate the gifts to Him, at the same time dedicate ourselves to Him as well.

Proper Attitudes for Worshipful Giving

A preacher left the pulpit one Sunday morning at offering time. Walking over to the usher who was taking the offering in the front row, the preacher looked over his shoulder and watched every coin which the people gave. Then he followed the usher down the aisle from row to row, noting what each person dropped into the plate. People were surprised, embarrassed, mad, and a few were amused. Back in the pulpit, he urged the congregation to forget that he had seen what each gave, but to remember that the sleepless eye of God was observing every gift.

Ushers, treasurers, and counting committees may see outward gifts, but the divine eye sees far more: motive, frequency, proportion, and any sacrifice. These intangibles,

fully known to God, show the measure of worshipfulness on the part of the giver. The Scriptures suggest certain criteria which make our offerings pleasing to God.

Giving Should Be Proportionate

Not only did God give us His only Son, but He continues to freely give us all things. Awareness of God's love-giving should awaken our desire to give back to Him. We can give without loving, but cannot love without giving. Giving to the Lord's work is economic evidence that we have been redeemed.

Not only should Christians give, but our giving should be proportionate to our income, and on a regular basis. Paul told the Corinthians, "Now concerning the collection for the saints, as I have given order to the churches of Galatia, even so do ye. Upon the first day of the week let everyone of you lay by him in store, as God hath prospered him, that there be no gatherings when I come" (1 Cor. 16:1-2). Though Paul referred to a particular collection for the poor saints at Jerusalem, he outlined several principles for giving.

First, everyone was to give, whether rich or poor. Second, offerings were to be made on the first day of the week, which means their day of worship must have been Sunday. Since the first day of the week commemorates the Resurrection of Christ, we should gladly bring our gifts to celebrate His victory over death.

Third, gifts were to be regular, not sporadic. It's so easy to fall into the habit of hit-and-miss giving. We tell ourselves we will give more when our income improves. Or we falsely assume we are giving more than we do. Unsystematic giving has a way of appearing far greater than it really is. The actual total would be shockingly low if an accurate record were kept by those who "generously" drop a bill on the plate once in a while.

Fourth, giving was to be proportionate, "as God hath prospered" each person (1 Cor. 16:2). The Jewish believers in Corinth, with all their Old Testament background, would

have understood that the proportion to be given was at the minimal a 10 percent. Those who today wish to abolish the standard of the tithe as legalistic should remember that the tithe was known long before the giving of the Law, for it was mentioned in connection with both Abraham and Jacob (Gen. 14:20; 28:22). Those who deny the validity of the tithe should not use their belief as an excuse for poor giving. The late Dr. Harry Ironside said, "The least a consistent child of God in Old Testament times could give was a tithe. Certainly, as a Christian living under grace, I shall not do less than was required of a consistent Jew. The tenth, therefore, will be the minimum, and I will give more according as God prospers me."

Giving Should Be Sincere

Isaiah warned of God's dislike of gifts coming from rebellious hearts. Wearied by the multitude of Israel's burnt offerings, the Lord's prime desire for them was to repent. "Wash you, make you clean; put away the evil of your doings from before Mine eyes; cease to do evil" (Isa. 1:16). The sacrifices that please God "are a broken spirit . . . and a contrite heart" (Ps. 51:17).

Our Lord is more interested in us than in our money. Paul commended the Corinthians who "first gave their own selves to the Lord" (2 Cor. 8:5). Unless we first present our bodies as living sacrifices to the Lord, our money-gifts will not be true worship. Some churches specifically invite only believers to support their work financially. I've heard announcements like this: "God's work should be supported by God's people. If you have been born again into God's family, we invite you to give as the offering plates are passed. If you are not a believer, we are not asking you to support God's work."

If you are about to make an offering to the Lord's work and recall a wrong you have inflicted on a fellow-believer, you should "leave there thy gift before the altar, and go thy way; first be reconciled to thy brother, and then come and offer thy gift" (Matt. 5:24).

The Lord wants us to give from the warmth of our hearts, not out of habit or with ulterior motives. Ananias and Sapphira were struck dead for pretending to give the total sale price of property when they actually gave only part (Acts 5:1-10). God knew their inner thoughts, just as He knows our thoughts.

Giving Should Be Cheerful

A little boy was given a quarter and a dime one Sunday morning with specific instructions to put the quarter on the plate at church, and to spend the dime on himself. Later he confessed, "I put the dime in church and spent the quarter on myself." Then he explained, "The preacher said the Lord loves a cheerful giver, and I felt much more cheerful about giving the dime."

Giving money must have caused pain to some in Paul's day, for he told the Corinthians to give "not grudgingly" (2 Cor. 9:7), which means literally, "not out of grief." Then he added, "Nor of necessity." Many people give because they feel they have to. They reason, *If I go to that service, they'll take an offering, and I'll have to give something.*

A funeral atmosphere prevails in most churches at offering time. But we are to give with the opposite attitude, "For God loveth a cheerful giver" (2 Cor. 9:7). The Greek word *cheerful* gives us our English word *hilarious.* Offering time should be a happy occasion. To ponder what God has done for us should make us "hilarious" givers.

Cheerfulness involves willingness. When materials were needed for the building of the tabernacle, the Lord instructed Moses, "Speak unto the Children of Israel, that they bring Me an offering; of every man that giveth it willingly with his heart ye shall take My offering" (Ex. 25:2). The result was that "they came, every one whose heart stirred him up, and every one whom his spirit made willing, and they brought the Lord's offering to the work of the tabernacle" (35:21). In fact, Moses had to restrain them from bringing any more gifts, so willingly did they give (36:6-7).

Incidentally, giving is a good criterion of one's mental health. According to Dr. Karl Menninger, "Generous people are rarely mentally ill people. Misers are miserable, whereas the generous are joyful" (Leslie Flynn, *Your God and Your Gold,* Zondervan, p. 94).

Giving Should Be Generous

Often we offer to God that which costs us little or nothing. Malachi rebuked the people because they offered to the Lord the blind, lame, and sick animals which were of little good to them (Mal. 1:8). Malachi reminded them they wouldn't offer sickly lambs to an earthly governor, so why should they offer them to God?

Teaching his seven-year-old girl the meaning of sacrifice, a father explained that the finest gift is some possession we value a great deal. On his birthday the father found pinned to his coat a large sheet of paper on which his daughter had printed with red crayon, "You are my faverit Daddy and I luv you heaps. My present to you is what I likes best. It's in your poket." In his pocket he found a strawberry lollipop he had given her a week before. It hadn't been licked once.

Zaccheus lived for himself and became rich. After meeting Jesus, he gave away half of his goods, besides restoring four-fold to all the people he had defrauded (Luke 19:2, 5, 8). Would many modern believers consider giving away half of their assets?

When Mary realized that Jesus was heading for the cross, she anointed Him with a costly box of alabaster, equivalent to a year's wages (John 12:3-7). She hadn't used it on her brother, Lazarus, when he died a little before this. Do we ever give an amount equal to a year's salary?

In the winter of 1981 the First Baptist Church of Atlanta, Georgia undertook the purchase of two large downtown city blocks, including the commercial buildings on the property, without borrowing any money. They were trusting God and not the mortgage bankers. With six days remaining till the deadline, only $125,000 had been given toward the cost of

$2.85 million. At the close of the first worship service, a young married couple walked the aisle during the invitation and told the pastor, Dr. Charles F. Stanley, that God had led them to give the wife's diamond wedding band. Their home had been recently burglarized, they explained, otherwise the gift would have been larger. Both insisted they had prayed about the decision and were sure that this was what God wanted them to do. When Dr. Stanley told the congregation at the second service of the couple's gift, the response was overwhelming. Members kept on bringing jewelry, titles to cars and motorcycles, other personal objects, and money for nearly an hour. But the church was still $1.5 million short. Dr. Stanley reminded the church members that their trust should be in God alone. Thirty minutes before the deadline, the church had raised all the money. The congregation praised God for His faithfulness and the sacrificial giving of hundreds of its members (Charles F. Stanley, *Handle with Prayer*, Victor, pp. 58-60).

The Bible encourages generous giving. "He which soweth sparingly shall reap also sparingly; and he which soweth bountifully shall reap also bountifully" (2 Cor. 9:6). Jesus said, "Give, and it shall be given unto you; good measure, pressed down, and shaken together, and running over, shall men give into your bosom. For with the same measure that ye mete withal it shall be measured to you again" (Luke 6:38).

Giving Should Be Expectant

If we would expect eternal dividends from our offerings, then our giving must be intelligent. Today's generous Christian public too often becomes gullible prey for anyone who publicizes a plausible story. We should give with caution, lest we pour money into the pockets of unscrupulous self-appointed prophets who live at the expense of tender-hearted saints. If an organization carries the seal of ECFA (the recently organized Evangelical Council for Financial Accountability), we know our gifts will be handled wisely.

We should give expectantly to bona fide projects, especially Bible-believing churches, confident that our dollars will be invested in spiritual treasure. Children will live godly lives because of Sunday School and youth groups. Adults will be won to Christ. Saints will be edified. People from foreign lands will be in heaven some day because of our missionary giving.

A sailor, shipwrecked on a South Sea island, was seized by the nationals, carried shoulder-high to a rude throne, and proclaimed king. He learned that according to their custom the king ruled for one year. The idea appealed to the sailor till he found out what happened when the year was up. When a king's reign ended, he was banished to a lonely island to starve to death. Knowing he was king for the year, the sailor began issuing orders. Farmers were sent to the island to plant crops. Carpenters made boats and a new home for the king. Ample food was transferred. When his reign finished, the sailor was exiled—not to a barren isle, but to a paradise of plenty.

Our Lord said, "Make to yourselves friends of the mammon of unrighteousness; that, when ye fail, they may receive you into everlasting habitations" (Luke 16:9). Worshipful, expectant giving will lay up treasure in heaven, where neither moth nor rust can corrupt, and where thieves cannot break through and steal (Matt. 6:19-20).

Giving Should Be to the Lord

A visitor in a large New York City church reached into his wallet at offering time and chose a $5 bill. Suddenly he recognized the usher coming his way as a well-known millionaire. Wishing to make a good impression, the giver switched the $5 for a $20 bill.

Jesus warned against giving gifts just to be seen of men (Matt. 6:1-2). The verb "to be seen" gives us our English word *theater*. Many play to the grandstand when they give. The Lord spoke humorously of a man blowing a trumpet before giving. Put in a modern setting, picture a man sitting

quietly in church till offering time. Then, as the plate approaches him, he stands up and pulls a trumpet out from under his coat, gives a few blasts, and when all are looking, drops a $20 bill on the plate. The Lord commented that when people applaud the giver, he has already gotten what he wanted, so he will not receive a reward in heaven. Rather than give for show, we are told to "let not thy left hand know what thy right hand doeth" (v. 3).

The day the poor widow quietly dropped her two mites into the temple treasury, rich men were ostentatiously dropping large sums into the same receptacle. But her seemingly unnoticed, tiny gift did not go unobserved by Jesus, nor will it go unrewarded (Luke 21:1-4).

In real worship our gifts are offered to the Triune God in response to all His wonderful gifts to us.

When the Saints Go Marching Out

12

In a treacherous area where boats frequently capsized on the rocks in bad weather, a harbor town was known for its faithful rescue team. Whenever the bell sounded, a group of men rowed quickly to the scene of disaster, risking their lives to remove sailors from sinking vessels or to pluck them from heaving waves.

After a few years the townsfolk collected money to build a rescue station near the shore to store all their equipment, thus making their rescue work easier. Also, special training was offered to others who wanted to become rescuers. The operation became quite efficient, saving hundreds from the raging waters.

But as time went by, comforts and conveniences were added to the building—including kitchen, cupboards full of food, dining room, lounge with thick carpet and stuffed chairs and recliners, and also sleeping quarters. The lovely building became a club where townspeople loved to eat, meet, play games, and socialize. The bell still sounded when a wreck occurred, but only a handful of people responded. Later, no one bothered to answer the rescue call, for they didn't wish to leave their creature comforts.

How easy it is for a country club mentality to seep into the

church, perverting its purpose and paralyzing its outreach. For many, "the service" has become the ringing of bells, the pomp of the processional, the flicker of candles, the resounding of the organ, the intonation of prayers, and the singing of hymns. But worship should never be allowed to become an escape from duty. Worship should lead to work. Adoration should initiate action. Worship, though a response to God, should result in service to man.

The close of the service is a very important moment. It's far better for the congregation to observe a few moments of silent meditation on what the service has meant to them, than to be getting ready to leave. Though friendly conversation and fellowship after a service should not be discouraged, the spiritual impact should not soon dissipate.

Service is related to and should result from worship. Our word *liturgy* comes from a Greek word which literally means "service" or the "work" of the people. In its verb form, *serve* is used interchangeably with the verb *worship* in the account of Jesus' temptation (Matt. 4:10). This word for "liturgy" is applied to the service of Zechariah in the temple (Luke 1:23), to collecting money for the poor at Jerusalem by the apostles (2 Cor. 9:12), and to the labors of Epaphroditus (Phil. 2:25).

Allegiance to God should not be measured only by attendance at church services, but by one's offering of self to a broken world. This may mean meeting in small groups for discipling, bearing one another's burdens, praying for one another, or taking a meal to a person who is sick. "Whether therefore ye eat, or drink, or whatsoever ye do, do all to the glory of God" (1 Cor. 10:31).

One reason for lack of consecration in many believers may be lack of worship. God seeks people to worship Him in spirit and in truth (John 4:24). This worship should then express itself in witness. Saints may not be serving because they have not been spiritually stimulated. Devotion in the church worship should motivate dedication for outside ministry.

A young man presented himself for membership at a distinguished New York City church. He said that, due to his busy schedule, he wanted to join a church where he could go on Sunday, listen to a fine sermon and good music, and not be called on to do anything. The pastor replied, "You are mistaken, young man. The church you want is up in the next block. It's called 'The Church of the Sacred Rest.' Here we have responsibilities which we expect our members to fulfill."

Sacrifices That Please God

From the beginning of history those who worshiped God brought offerings. The majority of Old Testament offerings were sacrifices, pointing forward to the Lamb of God who would take away the sin of the world. Since Jesus Christ offered Himself once for all as the perfect sacrifice for our sins, there no longer exists any need for blood sacrifice, as symbolized by the ripping of the curtain into the holy of holies (Heb. 9:24-28; 10:20).

However, Christians are enjoined to offer sacrifices to the Lord in worship. Peter calls believers "an holy priesthood, to offer up spiritual sacrifices, acceptable to God by Jesus Christ" (1 Peter 2:5). These sacrifices in no way take the place of Christ's death on the cross. Rather, the sacrifices of believers are made in response to His supreme, eternal sacrifice. Because He made such a sacrifice, unrepeatable and efficacious, we want to say thanks by making sacrifices. Since we don't offer sacrifices like God's ancient people, what are these "spiritual sacrifices" which please Him?

Sacrifice of Praise

We are commanded, "Let us offer the sacrifice of praise to God continually, that is, the fruit of our lips giving thanks to His name" (Heb. 13:15). Whenever we tell about God's goodness, we are offering the sacrifice of praise.

Whenever we sing the praises of God and of His Christ, privately or in public worship, we are offering the fruit of our

lips. Mere singing doesn't necessarily constitute acceptable sacrifice. The words must be the deep-down response of our spirit to the matchless grace of God, not the mumbling of mere repetition. The psalmist says, "I will offer in His tabernacle sacrifices of joy; I will sing, yea, I will sing praises unto the Lord (27:6).

This sacrifice of praise is to be offered outside the church in everyday experiences. We tend to blame God when things go wrong, and praise Him only when they go right. But we are to give thanks in everything. Job, who lost livestock, children, and health reacted with praise, "'The Lord gave, and the Lord hath taken away; blessed be the name of the Lord.' In all this Job sinned not, nor charged God foolishly" (Job 1:21-22).

A mother, whose missionary son had been killed in a plane crash in Africa, wrote the mission board. "It was a great shock to receive the news of his tragic death. I asked the Western Union girl to read the telegram again. She read, 'Plane crashed January 12th. Your son in glory.' I said to the girl, 'Praise the Lord.' She wanted to know what 'in glory' meant. So I told her that my son was with the Lord. She said, 'I'm so sorry to hear that.' But I answered, 'Well, there's no use being sorry. God's way is the best way. And we know God never makes a mistake. Blessed be His holy name!' She wondered how I could take it the way I did. I told her it was through God's sufficient grace." That mother indeed offered the sacrifice of praise.

Sacrifice of a Broken Heart

King Saul, disobeying divine instructions by failing to slaughter all sheep in a war with the Agagites, excused his action by saying he intended to offer them as sacrifices to the Lord. The Prophet Samuel replied, "Hath the Lord as great delight in burnt offerings and sacrifices, as in obeying the voice of the Lord? Behold, to obey is better than sacrifice, and to hearken than the fat of rams" (1 Sam. 15:22). To the hard-hearted Pharisees the Lord said, "I will have mercy, and not

sacrifice" (Matt. 9:13). The Lord would rather have the sacrifice of contrite obedience than a big donation given with stubborn disobedience.

After his double sin of adultery and murder, David must have presented sacrifices for about a year. Yet all the time he was unrepentant of his heinous deeds. Bringing sacrifice after sacrifice as though all were well in his relationship with the Lord, David needed divine confrontation. So God sent His Prophet Nathan to convict the king. When David realized his burden of sin, he cried out in repentance, "Against Thee, Thee only, have I sinned. . . . Purge me with hyssop and I shall be clean. . . . The sacrifices of God are a broken spirit; a broken and a contrite heart, O God, Thou wilt not despise" (Ps. 51:4, 7, 17). David ended his psalm of penitence, "Then shalt Thou be pleased with the sacrifices of righteousness" (v. 19).

Sacrifice of Material Things

When Paul thanked the Philippians for a gift they had sent him, he called it "an odor of a sweet smell, a sacrifice acceptable, well pleasing to God" (Phil. 4:18). Whenever a believer shares from his heart his material substance with a person in need, he is making an acceptable offering to the Lord. "To do good and to communicate forget not, for with such sacrifices God is well pleased" (Heb. 13:16).

A man was packing a shipment of food contributed by a school for the poor people in Appalachia. He was separating beans from powdered milk, and canned vegetables from canned meats. Reaching into a box filled with various cans, he pulled out a little brown paper sack. Apparently one of the pupils had brought something different from the items on the suggested list. Out of the paper bag fell a peanut butter sandwich, an apple, and a cookie. Crayoned in large letters was a little girl's name, "Christy—Room 104." She had given up her lunch for some hungry person. The Lord delights in sacrifices of material things to help the less fortunate.

Sacrifice of Good Works

The same verse which tells us to share our material goods also commands us "to do good . . . for with such sacrifices God is well pleased" (Heb. 13:16). Though good works never provide eternal salvation, the saved are expected to do good works (Eph. 2:8-10; Titus 3:5-8). Performed out of gratitude for the once-for-all sacrifice of Christ, these good works become spiritual sacrifices acceptable to God.

Moses' worship at the burning bush was followed by his good work of leading the Israelites out of Egyptian bondage. Mary's worship at the feet of Jesus led her to anoint Him with expensive perfume in anticipation of His burial (John 12:3-8).

Genuine worship not only involves our minds in contemplation, and stirs our hearts in love, but also moves our feet to service. It means ministering to a hungry and hurting world. Pure religion (worship as expressed in ritual acts) includes visitation and assistance to widows and orphans (James 1:27). Even the fulfilling of our duties as mates, children, parents, employees, or employers (Col. 3:18—4:1) can be considered sacrifices "well pleasing unto the Lord" (3:20).

Sacrifice of Loved Ones

Though Abraham loved his son Isaac dearly, he valued God more. Abraham proved his love for God by his willingness to sacrifice his only son (Gen. 22:1-13). Hannah, becoming a mother after years of barrenness, brought a tremendous sacrifice—her only son—to the tabernacle. She gave Samuel back to the Lord to live at the tabernacle permanently (1 Sam. 1:20-28). Jesus said, "He that loveth father or mother more than Me is not worthy of Me: and he that loveth son or daughter more than Me is not worthy of Me" (Matt. 10:37). Jesus reproached a would-be disciple because he put duty to his earthly father above duty to God (Luke 9:59-60).

Many young people, faced with an eviction order from their parents unless they deny their Christian profession,

have chosen Christ. Some faithful youths have been disowned by their parents, or disinherited, or considered dead. One young man reported that his parents refused to ever see him again, and would cross the street to avoid him.

Sacrifice of Our Bodies

In his letter to the Romans, Paul urged believers to make the ultimate sacrifices, "I beseech you therefore, brethren, by the mercies of God, that ye present your bodies a living sacrifice, holy, acceptable unto God, which is your reasonable service" (12:1).

Paul appreciated not only the material offering for the poor at Jerusalem which the Macedonians were making, but also the offering of their persons. He said of them, "This they did . . . but first gave their own selves to the Lord" (2 Cor. 8:5).

Though we may not be called on to actually lay down our lives, our willingness to do so would make us virtually living-dead persons. Paul was a living-dead individual. He didn't enjoy the beatings, nor did he like hunger, thirst, shipwreck, and all the privations which he suffered. Because he was a living sacrifice, he was a bondslave—dead to his own ambitions—but alive to the Lord's plans.

Before the Dieppe raid of World War II, an English civilian with the code name "Professor Wendell" received an unusual assignment. Because of his inventions in radio detection, the Royal Air Force was always able to spot German planes before they reached their targets. With the invasion of the continent imminent, the Allies needed to learn what kind of installations the enemy had by the shores. Professor Wendell was assigned to investigate a radio detection finder near Dieppe.

When the regiment landed quietly, no enemy was in sight. With Professor Wendell's vast technical knowledge, he would only need a few minutes of examination. Most of the soldiers trained their guns in the direction of any potential enemy. But the professor had a bodyguard of four soldiers

whose only job was to keep their drawn guns on him. If the enemy surprised the expedition, the four soldiers had orders to shoot, not the enemy, but the professor. By no means was this genius of radio detection to fall into enemy hands. As a volunteer for this dangerous assignment, the professor was a living sacrifice.

A boy asked an old saint, "What does it mean to be crucified?" The saint replied, "It means three things. One—a man on the cross faced only one direction. Two—he was not going back anywhere. Three—he had no further plans of his own."

In the early days of the West, a missionary came to a little Indian village. The people gradually assembled in the center, among them their chief—a tall, handsome man. The missionary's message was simple, but powerful. After awhile, the chief arose, walked to the front, and looking the missionary squarely in the eye, said, "Big Chief give tomahawk to Jesus." The truth of God's desire for peace had gotten through. Later the chief walked to the front again, this time saying, "Big Chief give robe to Jesus." He returned to his seat. Finally, the chief came forward a third time. This time he said, "Big Chief give self to Jesus."

The Lord does want the sacrifices of our praise, a broken spirit, material things, good works, and personal idols—but most of all, He wants our own lives.

All these sacrifices come as a response to worship. At the end of Isaiah's vision of God came the divine invitation to service, "Whom shall I send, and who will go for us?" Then Isaiah volunteered, "Here am I; send me" (Isa. 6:8). Worship is related to missions. The Lord says, "Come unto Me. Learn of Me. Be like Me." Then, "Go for Me into all the world." Worshiping merely for personal fulfillment or a spiritual high is insufficient and selfish. Contemplating must lead to communicating. The church's worship and witness cannot be separated. Transformed into His likeness, we should "show forth the praises of Him who hath called you out of darkness into His marvelous light" (1 Peter 2:9).

A Turkish officer attacked an Armenian home, murdered the elderly parents, permitted his soldiers to rape the daughters, but kept the eldest girl for himself, forcing her to live with him. She later escaped and entered a nursing school. A few years later she found herself nursing in a ward of Turkish officers. One night, lifting her lantern toward a patient's bed, she looked into the face of this officer. He was too ill to recognize her. She knew that unless he received unusual nursing care he would die. As the days passed, he improved. One day the doctor, standing by the officer's bed, said, "But for this nurse's skillful devotion to you, you'd be in your grave." The officer looked at her, "You look familiar. Haven't we met before?" Learning her identity, he asked, "Why didn't you kill me?" She replied, "I am a follower of Him who said, 'Love your enemies.'"

A visitor in a European city noticed on a high wall the stone figure of a lamb. A local resident informed him that it marked the place from which a workman fell when the building was under construction. However, the workman miraculously was not killed. When fellow workers hurried down to find his broken body on the ground, they found him alive, though shaken and bruised, with hardly a bone broken. As the workman fell, a line of lambs was on the way to the slaughter. He landed on the back of one of them, killing the lamb who broke his fall. The builder was so impressed that he had the stone lamb placed on the wall as a permanent reminder. With infinitely greater wonder heavenly creatures, angelic choirs, the redeemed, and all creation behold the Father and the Lamb on the throne in heaven.

The many songs in the Book of Revelation indicate there will be much worship in glory. Chapters 4 and 5 of Revelation constitute a great oratorio in 2 sections. Part 1 deals with creation; part 2 with redemption. Around the throne 4 living creatures rest neither day nor night, praising, "Holy, holy, holy, Lord God Almighty, which was, and is, and is to come" (4:8). Joining this quartet is a choir of 24 elders, falling down before the Father, casting their crowns before Him,

and praising Him for His *creative* power, "Thou art worthy, O Lord, to receive glory and honor and power; for Thou hast created all things, and for Thy pleasure they are and were created" (v. 11).

When the Lamb also appears in the midst of the throne, the quartet of living creatures and the choir of 24 elders fall down before the Lamb and sing a new *redemptive* song, "Thou art worthy to take the Book . . . for Thou wast slain, and hast redeemed us to God by Thy blood out of every kindred, and tongue, and people, and nation" (5:9). Then countless angels join the praise, "Worthy is the Lamb that was slain to receive power, and riches, and wisdom, and strength, and honor, and glory, and blessing" (v. 12). Finally, all creation in grand finale joins the others in adoration of both Father and Son, "Blessing, and honor, and glory, and power be unto Him that sitteth upon the throne, and unto the Lamb forever and ever" (v. 13).

Worship can never lose sight of the Lamb that was slain. The Lord Jesus is the supreme revelation of the Father whereby through the Spirit we are made nigh to the throne. To ponder Him dying on the cross is to assure ourselves of the Father's love which sent His Son to bear our sins away. Then someday we'll join that countless choir in the glory land of worship.

Additional books written by Leslie Flynn include:

The Gift of Joy

How do you find joy? How are joy and happiness related? How are they different? In this book, Dr. Flynn dispels the myths that joy equals happiness and that grumpiness equals holiness.

God's Will: You Can Know It

How do you go about finding God's will? How can you be a decisive person—yet at the same time know you are following God's leading? From biblical principles—and the experiences of people of the past and present—you can learn how to let God direct you.

Joseph: God's Man in Egypt

Joseph was a perfect candidate for anger, despair, revenge, and self-pity. Yet Joseph's life offers hope—you too can live with courage and faith when everything around you goes wrong.

19 Gifts of the Spirit

Examine the gifts and special abilities given to Christians by the Holy Spirit. Which ones do you have? Are you using them? Dr. Flynn guides you in an in-depth study of what the Bible says about spiritual gifts.

Dare to Care Like Jesus

You can develop greater compassion as you follow the example Jesus set in His tears, anger, patience, gratitude, approachability, loneliness, humor, submissiveness, and graciousness.

The Twelve

What were the disciples like before they met Jesus? How did He change them? In this book, you'll discover the unvarnished truth about the 12 ordinary men Jesus chose.

WORSHIP:
TOGETHER WE CELEBRATE